Echoes of Eternity:

Potana's Spiritual Awakening

by

Venkat Potana

Purpose

In penning *Echoes of Eternity: Bhakta Potana's Spiritual Awakening*, I seek not to exalt myself but to give all glory to Almighty God for the remarkable journey He has orchestrated in my life. Each chapter, marked by trials and triumphs, is a testament to His unwavering faithfulness and grace. It is through His divine guidance that I have experienced transformation, fulfillment, and purpose, and I hope that my story serves as an encouragement to readers everywhere. Trusting the Lord has been the cornerstone of my journey, and it is my prayer that those who read these pages will be inspired to place their faith in Him, knowing that He is capable of achieving far more than we can ask or imagine. All the achievements and milestones documented here are not mine but are a reflection of God's love and provision, and I give Him all the praise and honor for what He has done in my life.

Dr. Venkat Potana
9/30/2024.

About the Author

Dr. Venkat Potana holds a Ph.D. from the University of Mysore through ***South Asia Institute of Advanced Christian Studies*** (SAIACS), Bangalore, with international exposure at Yale Divinity School, CT, Fuller Theological Seminary, LA, in the USA. He graduated in English literature from Acharya Nagarjuna University and earned a master's in social work from the same university. He also has another master's degree in Religion and Philosophy from Madurai Kamaraj University. He received his Master of Divinity from GFA Seminary. He also received a Master of Theology (Th.M.) degree at Union Biblical Seminary.

Dr. Potana is a professor of Missiology/ Theology, a writer, a Social Worker, and a scholar, among many other things. He has authored several Missiology textbooks and published plentiful scholarly articles in international journals. At present, he teaches at EUCON International University, MP, Saipan, USA.

Dedication

To my beloved parents,

Potana Nancharaiah and Manikayala Devi,

Though no longer with me in this life, your presence remains in every breath I take. My father, whose short-term absence shaped my deepest longing for love, and my mother, whose resilience and unwavering faith became the foundation of my strength. Your stories of sacrifice, hardship, and hope are woven into every page of my life. This journey, with all its trials and triumphs, is as much yours as it is mine.

With deepest love and gratitude,

Dr. Venkat Potana

Contents

About the Book

"Echoes of Eternity: Bhakta Potana's Spiritual Awakening" is a deeply personal and transformative journey of faith, set against the backdrop of a rich Hindu heritage and cultural traditions. Through this autobiography, Bhakta Potana shares the profound experiences that shaped his life, from a childhood marked by hardship and spiritual longing to an eventual encounter with the living Christ that forever changed his destiny.

Raised amidst the tension of Vaishnavite and Shaivite religious practices, the author navigates the complexities of ancestral legacies, family conflicts, and personal struggles. The narrative captures his early years spent searching for meaning and divine intervention, culminating in a miraculous vision of Almighty God that redefined his understanding of faith, purpose, and peace. With vivid memories of family, tradition, and spiritual battles, *Echoes of Eternity* is not just a memoir but a demonstration of the power of grace, redemption, and the call to a higher spiritual truth.

This book invites readers on a reflective

pilgrimage, encouraging them to seek their own spiritual awakening, while offering insight into the universal search for Almighty God across cultural and religious boundaries. Written with the hope of inspiring others to experience the same divine transformation, it is a powerful testimony of faith in the midst of life's trials.

Foreword

When I first met **Dr. Venkat**, I was struck by his quiet strength, humble demeanor, and deep sense of purpose. Little did I know then the journey he had taken to become the man he is today—a journey filled with pain, sacrifice, and an unyielding search for truth. As his wife, I've had the privilege of walking with him through many seasons of life, and I've witnessed firsthand the faith and perseverance that have shaped his character and his commitment to God.

Growing up, Dr. Venkat faced circumstances that would have broken many. As a child, he dealt with the neglect of his father, forcing him to navigate life's challenges at a tender age. His early years were defined by hardship—working from dawn to dusk, striving for an education with little support, and enduring the pain of loss and rejection. Yet, despite all of this, he carried within him a quiet hope, a sense that there was something greater waiting for him, a purpose beyond the suffering.

It was this hope, this relentless search for meaning, that led him to Christ. I remember him telling me about the pivotal moments in his life when he called out to God, seeking comfort and answers. It wasn't easy for him to turn away from the traditions he was raised in, nor was it without consequence. But in those moments, as he chose to embrace the Christian faith, he found the peace and purpose he had longed for. His decision to follow Christ was not just an emotional experience—it was a lifelong commitment, one that shaped everything he did thereafter.

As his wife, I've had the honor of seeing the impact of his faith on the lives of others. Whether in the workplace, at home, or among friends, he has always been a beacon of encouragement and inspiration. His story is one of transformation—of how God's grace can take the most challenging circumstances and turn them into testimonies of hope. He embodies resilience, not because life has been easy, but because he has learned to rely on God's strength rather than his own.

Writing this autobiography was no easy task for him. It required revisiting painful memories and opening up about struggles that he had long kept private. But in doing so, he has allowed others to see the full picture of God's work in his life. This book is more than a recounting of events—it is a declaration of faith, a testament to the power of perseverance, and a reflection of God's grace at work in the life of one man. As I read through the pages of his story, I was moved not only by the challenges he faced but also by the unwavering commitment he had to honor God through it all. He never allowed bitterness or resentment to take root in his heart. Instead, he chose love, forgiveness, and faith. I believe that anyone who reads this autobiography will be deeply touched by the authenticity and transparency with which he shares his journey.

To those who pick up this book, I want you to know that the man behind these words is the same man I am blessed to call my husband—a man of integrity, humility, and unwavering faith. His life is a living testimony to the transformative power of God's love, and I pray that as you read his story, you are inspired to trust in God's plan for your own life.

Mrs. Rita Potana, 9/29/2024.

Preface

The journey of life is often one of endless questioning, a search for meaning that transcends the material and temporal world we inhabit. For me, this journey began in my earliest years, when a deep-seated longing to understand the Almighty and experience the divine essence filled my heart. Growing up in a devout environment, I was immersed in prayers and rituals, offering devotion to the pantheon of gods in our tradition. Yet, despite my fervent piety, I could not shake the feeling that something crucial was missing. The existential questions that troubled me—about the nature of life, the purpose of existence, and my place in this vast cosmos—remained unanswered. This sense of incompletion propelled me forward, deepening my search for the ultimate truth.

It was not a smooth or linear path. The quest to know the Almighty is often fraught with confusion, doubt, and challenges. While I sought answers through devotion and prayer, my soul was restless. I desired more than intellectual understanding; I wanted to experience the divine personally, to feel the living presence of the Supreme in my life. This yearning stayed with me through my youth, driving me to explore all avenues of spiritual knowledge available to me. Yet, the more I searched, the more elusive the answers seemed.

Everything changed in 1993, when, at the age of 19, I experienced a profound turning point. While reading a passage from the ancient text of Jeremiah 1:4-10, I felt as though the Lord himself spoke to me. It was a moment that transcended the boundaries of intellectual understanding; it was an experience that touched the very core of my being. I heard the voice of the divine, not as a distant entity, but as a loving, guiding presence. It was as if the Almighty was speaking to me directly, as a father would speak to his beloved child. In that moment, I realized that the answers I had been searching for could not be found through ritual or reason alone—they had to be revealed through grace.

The clarity of that encounter was overwhelming. For years, I had sought the divine with all my heart, and now, the Almighty had revealed Himself to me in a way that was deeply personal and transformative. On August 7, 1993, I had what could only be described as a *darshan* of the Supreme. At that moment, all my doubts and fears were shattered. I no longer needed to search; the truth was laid bare before me. The Almighty was not a distant, abstract concept but a living presence who could be experienced and known intimately. This experience marked the beginning of a new chapter in my life, one in which I would devote myself to living in alignment with the divine will.

Though I had been raised with a deep respect for the rich spiritual heritage of my ancestors, the revelation I received from the Almighty reshaped my understanding of faith. Coming from an upper-caste Hindu background, I initially found it challenging to reconcile my cultural and social identity with the newfound path I had embarked upon. Indian society is complex, with its own intricate dynamics and deeply ingrained traditions. Like many, I was shaped by the caste consciousness that pervades much of our culture. However, the divine, in His infinite wisdom, showed me that true spirituality transcends all social divisions. The Supreme does not look at caste, creed, or background; the divine call is to every soul, irrespective of these earthly distinctions. This realization was liberating, allowing me to embrace a more expansive understanding of the Almighty, one that went beyond the confines of traditional boundaries.

As I continued my studies at university, this newfound relationship with the divine began to take on a larger role in my life. I was not content to keep these experiences to myself. The joy and peace that I had found were too profound to be contained. I felt a strong calling to share this wisdom and insight with others, particularly with my fellow students, who, like me, were often grappling with the deeper questions of life. During my time in Tenali, Andhra Pradesh, I became actively involved in spiritual discussions and gatherings. Through these encounters, I had the privilege of witnessing the transformative power of the divine in the lives of others as well.

The examples of the great sages and leaders from our sacred texts—such as Moses and Abraham—became powerful sources of inspiration for me. These figures were not just historical or mythological; they were embodiments of what it meant to live in alignment with the divine purpose. Their journeys of faith and discovery resonated with my own, reminding me that the path of spiritual awakening is often one of trials, tests, and growth. It was through their stories that I came to understand that my own life had been set apart for a special purpose. I felt a deep sense of calling to serve as a guide and witness to others, helping them discover the divine in their own lives.

This calling took me to many places, and over the course of fourteen years, I dedicated myself to working with university students across India. My work primarily focused on helping young people, who, like myself, were seeking answers to the great questions of life. My involvement with the Union of Evangelical Students of India (UESI) provided me with the opportunity to share the insights and wisdom that I had gained through my spiritual journey. In the hills of Uttarakhand and across the campuses of both North and South India, I sought to encourage students to cultivate their own relationship with the divine and to live lives of integrity, compassion, and service to society.

During this period, I was fortunate enough to

witness countless lives being touched by the divine. Through retreats, study groups, and spiritual gatherings, students came to experience a deeper connection with the Almighty. Many of them went on to become leaders in their own right, serving both the spiritual and material needs of their communities. As someone who had come from a Hindu background, I was uniquely positioned to help bridge the gap between the spiritual traditions of my youth and the broader, more inclusive understanding of the divine that I had come to embrace.

This journey of spiritual growth also led me to pursue higher education, where I explored the deeper aspects of religious thought and philosophy. My PhD research at SAIACS, Bangalore, through the University of Mysore, along with international exposure at institutions like Yale Divinity School and Fuller Theological Seminary in the USA, broadened my understanding of both Eastern and Western spiritual traditions. Through these academic pursuits, I sought to deepen my own faith and contribute to the wider body of knowledge regarding spirituality and the human experience.

Today, as I reflect on the many years that have passed since that life-changing moment in 1993, I am filled with gratitude. I have been blessed with a loving family—my wife, Rita, and our three wonderful children, Sophia, Lydia, and Ashish Vidwan. My academic work continues to inspire me, and I am privileged to serve as a professor of theology at EUCON International University. But more than any personal or professional achievement, it is the knowledge of the divine presence in my life that brings me the greatest joy. The Almighty has led me through many seasons of life, and it is my hope that through this autobiography, *Echoes of Eternity: Bhakta Potana's Spiritual Awakening*, others may find inspiration to seek and experience the eternal truth for themselves.

In sharing my story, I aim not only to recount the significant events of my life but also to offer a reflection on the universal spiritual journey—a journey that transcends cultural, religious, and social barriers. The divine call is open to all, and it is my prayer that each reader will feel encouraged to embark on their own path of discovery, wherever it may lead.

Throughout this book, I share the struggles and

triumphs of my life—not to highlight my own strength, but to show how God's strength carried me through every trial. From the challenges of growing up with a lot of challenges to the difficulties of pursuing an education against all odds to the profound spiritual experiences that forever changed my path, every chapter is a reflection of God's work in my life. There were many moments when I thought I couldn't go on, but time and again, God showed me that His plans were greater than my own and that His timing was perfect.

I want to make it clear that my story is not unique. Every one of us faces challenges, heartaches, and moments when we feel abandoned or lost. But I firmly believe that it is in those moments that God is closest to us, even when we can't see it. Through my journey, I hope to inspire you to hold on to hope, to trust in God's plan for your life, and to believe that no matter how difficult the road may seem, there is a purpose to your pain, and a divine plan waiting to unfold.

As you read this book, I invite you to reflect on your own journey. Perhaps you will see parallels between my struggles and your own. Perhaps you will be reminded of moments when you, too, called out for divine help. Wherever you find yourself, my prayer is that this story will encourage you to press on, to trust in God's faithfulness, and to embrace the truth that He is always with you.

I did not set out to write this autobiography simply to share my life story. I wrote it with a purpose—to show how God can take even the most difficult circumstances and turn them into opportunities for growth, transformation, and spiritual awakening. My desire is that through these pages, you will find inspiration to deepen your relationship with God, to seek Him in the midst of your struggles, and to walk in the assurance that His love and grace are more than enough.

I am eternally grateful for the people who have been a part of my journey—those who stood by me in difficult times, and those who encouraged me to keep moving forward. Above all, I am thankful to God, whose mercy and love have sustained me through every season of life. Without Him, none of this would have been possible. So, as you begin this journey with me, I encourage you to open your heart, not just to my story, but to the possibility of seeing God's hand in your own life.

With sincere thanks,

Dr. Venkat Potana 8/28/2024.

Introduction

Life is a tapestry woven from moments of joy, pain, faith, and transformation. As we journey through it, we often search for meaning beyond the mundane, striving to understand the divine purpose that guides us. My story, *Echoes of Eternity: Bhakta Potana's Spiritual Awakening*, is the account of such a journey—a journey that has taken me from the heart of tradition and struggle to an encounter with divine grace that forever altered my life.

I was born into a family rich in spiritual heritage, where the echoes of Shaivite and Vaishnavite devotion reverberated through generations. However, my path was not always one of clarity. From early childhood, marked by family conflicts to near-death experiences my life has been a constant search for peace and purpose. It was within this turmoil that I first felt the stirrings of a higher calling—a calling that would reveal itself through miraculous moments of divine protection and profound spiritual encounters.

In this autobiography, I share the pivotal moments that shaped me—from the pain of poverty to the joy of spiritual awakening. This is not simply a recollection of past events, but a testament to the unwavering grace of Almighty God. My journey led me through periods of doubt, hardship, and struggle, but always with the guiding hand of divine intervention shaping my path. Each chapter is a reflection of how the Almighty transformed my trials into triumphs and my uncertainty into unwavering faith.

Through the experiences I recount, my hope is to inspire others who find themselves grappling with their own life's challenges. No matter how difficult the circumstances, there is always a divine plan at work—a higher purpose that we may not always understand, but which becomes clear through faith. In sharing my story, I wish to offer encouragement and hope to those seeking spiritual awakening and personal transformation.

May the echoes of eternity that I have experienced resound in your heart, inviting you to explore the depths of your own spiritual journey.

1. Ancestral Roots

Our heritage forms the foundation of who we are, often influencing the trajectory of our lives in ways we cannot fully comprehend. In my journey, the intertwined legacies of my ancestors laid the groundwork for my spiritual quest, offering both blessings and challenges. This section delves into the rich and complex narratives of my forefathers—particularly the Shaivite devotion of my paternal lineage and the Vaishnavite faith of my maternal side. These two streams of Hindu spirituality, though united under the larger umbrella of the same faith, brought tension and discord within the family, but also shaped my early understanding of religion and devotion.

My paternal grandfather, Potana Lakshmi Narayana, was a dedicated Shaivite ascetic, whose life was marked by austerity and profound mystical experiences. His decision to leave behind material comforts for a life of renunciation profoundly impacted the spiritual landscape of my family, leaving a lasting legacy of devotion and asceticism.

On the other hand, my maternal grandfather,

Chinnam Rathaiah, a devout Vaishnavite, embodied a different form of faith, one rooted in disciplined worship of Lord Vishnu. His struggles to find peace amidst a life of devotion reflect the challenges of aligning human desires with spiritual fulfillment.

The conflict between these two religious traditions was not merely philosophical but became a source of deep familial strife, shaping the lives and decisions of my parents and, in turn, my own. Understanding these ancestral roots helps to uncover the foundations of my spiritual awakening, and how the divine plan was at work long before I was aware of it.

1.1 Paternal Shaivite Heritage

Potana Lakshmi Narayana, a name etched with respect and reverence in his native region, hailed from the quaint village of Bhatlapenumarru in Krishna District, Andhra Pradesh. Known for its historical significance, particularly as the birthplace of Pingali Venkayya,

the designer of the Indian flag, Bhatlapenumarru was a place where tradition and modernity coexisted harmoniously. In this setting, Lakshmi Narayana grew up amidst a backdrop of cultural richness and spiritual heritage. From a young age, Lakshmi Narayana exhibited an uncommon depth of spirituality. His upbringing in a village known for its connection to significant historical figures instilled in him a profound appreciation for both the material and the metaphysical. Despite the comforts and privileges afforded by his affluent family, he felt a calling that transcended the mundane aspects of his life.

Lakshmi Narayana's life took a drastic negative turning point while on a journey to a famous south Indian Hindu temple, Bhramaramba Devi-Srisailam Temple. This pilgrimage was interpreted by him not merely as a religious duty but as a journey into the heart of spiritual awakening. As he wandered through the forest grounds, seeking divine blessings and solace, he experienced a moment of revelation. It was during this pilgrimage that Lakshmi Narayana received a message from the spirits. In a moment of deep meditation and prayer, he heard a spirit's (*Devata*) instructions—an unequivocal directive to forgo all physical sustenance and dedicate his life to contemplation. This spirit's instruction was clear and unambiguous, urging him to abandon his worldly possessions and immerse himself entirely in spiritual practice. The message was a negative turning point that reshaped his life's tragedy. The idea of living without food, focusing solely on meditation and spiritual growth, was a radical departure from his current existence. Yet, Lakshmi Narayana, deeply moved by the spirit's command, resolved to heed this calling, setting the stage for a life marked by profound transformation.

Upon his return from pilgrimage to Bhatlapenumarru, his native town, Lakshmi Narayana began the process of disentangling himself from the material world. He sold his possessions, relinquished his wealth, and distanced himself from his family and social circles. The decision was not merely physical but a complete mental and emotional detachment from the luxuries that had once defined his existence. His quest for solitude led him to search for an appropriate location that would serve as his sanctuary. After considerable exploration, Lakshmi Narayana settled on a remote forest area in Koya Venkaiah Banjara, a village within the Panchayat of Pangidi, located in the Raghunadhaspalem Mandal of Khammam District. This forest, dense and secluded, offered the isolation he sought for his spiritual practices.

The acquisition of twenty-five acres of this wilderness marked the beginning of his new life. The land, untouched and primal, was a stark contrast to the developed and bustling environment of Krishna District. Here, Lakshmi Narayana built a modest dwelling and established a simple, hut, space for meditation and reflection. At forty years of age, he arrived at this village in the forest, marking the beginning of a more austere chapter in his life. With the physical transition complete, Lakshmi Narayana embarked on the most challenging phase of his spiritual journey—ceasing all food intake. At the age of forty, he made the extraordinary decision to live without sustenance, dedicating his entire existence to meditation and spiritual pursuit. As for me, this choice was a reckless abandonment and a deliberate act of foolishness, intended to transcend the limitations of the physical body and attain a higher spiritual state.

Living in solitude, Lakshmi Narayana's days were filled with rigorous meditation and contemplative practices. His life in the forest was marked by simplicity and austerity. He constructed a modest hut using natural materials, ensuring that his surroundings remained in harmony with the environment. His daily routine involved prolonged periods of meditation, prayer, and self-reflection, with minimal interaction with the outside world. His ascetic lifestyle drew the curiosity and respect of local villagers and pilgrims. Although his choice to abstain from food was unusual and extreme, it was seen as a demonstration of his unwavering commitment to spiritual enlightenment to the outside world. The forest around him became a sacred space, and his presence began to imbue it with an aura of mysticism.

As Lakshmi Narayana's spiritual practice deepened, he began to experience a series of mystical phenomena that further cemented his reputation as a revered ascetic. The forest, once a mere expanse of trees and silence, became a locus of spiritual miracles. Locals and visitors alike reported witnessing inexplicable events, attributing them to the divine grace that seemed to flow through Lakshmi Narayana. One of the most remarkable stories involved a divine light that was said to envelop him during meditation. Witnesses described it as a celestial radiance, illuminating not just the physical space but also the spiritual essence of the surroundings. This phenomenon was interpreted as a direct manifestation of divine presence, affirming his status as a spiritual beacon. As the years went by, Potana Lakshmi Narayana's life turned into a powerful example of the transformational power of asceticism and the strength of spiritual determination. His legacy, intertwined with the mystical experiences he embodied, left an indelible mark on the hearts and minds of those who encountered him. His forest sanctuary, once a remote and unassuming plot of land, became a revered place of pilgrimage and spiritual significance.

A Spiritual Beacon and a Struggle for Peace

As I described, my grandfather, Potana Lakshminarayana, was regarded by many as a spiritual figure of deep significance. People saw in him an ascetic who had attained a level of spiritual enlightenment that few could imagine. His commitment to spiritual practices, which many believed to be a direct manifestation of divine presence, marked him as a man deeply connected to the sacred. His name was often spoken with reverence, and people from far and near would seek his counsel and blessings. In a world that often feels disconnected from the divine, he stood out as a beacon of spirituality and wisdom.

However, beneath this revered image lay a much more complicated reality. While people interpreted his lifestyle as an affirmation of divine grace, this narrative often overshadowed the personal sacrifices and struggles that accompanied his spiritual journey. It is easy to admire someone for their outward expressions of faith and dedication, but those who knew him closely, especially his family, were aware of the significant costs that his spiritual devotion had on his personal life.

In pursuing a life that many saw as spiritually exalted, my grandfather neglected some of the fundamental aspects of family life. His focus on the divine and his ascetic practices came at the expense of fulfilling the responsibilities that come with being a husband, father, and grandfather. There was a disconnect between the revered figure people saw and the man who, in his later years, faced deep regret for the choices he had made.

My Grandfather's Struggles

As a young boy, I often observed my grandfather from a distance, watching as he navigated his daily life. To the outside world, he may have seemed like a man in perfect harmony with his spiritual path, but to those closest to him, the cracks in this facade were clear. I remember moments when his struggles were palpable. There was an underlying tension in his life, a certain heaviness in the way he carried himself, that was impossible to ignore.

In many ways, my grandfather was a man torn between two worlds. On one hand, he was deeply committed to his spiritual path, which required a level of detachment from the material world. On the other hand, he was part of a family, with obligations and responsibilities that could not be ignored. As a child, I did not fully understand the complexities of his inner turmoil, but I could sense that he was not at peace.

I often witnessed him in states of quiet

contemplation, as though searching for something he could not find. His ascetic practices, which were meant to bring him closer to a sense of divine peace, seemed to only deepen his internal conflict. The peace that he sought so fervently through his spiritual practices remained elusive, and this created a tension that permeated the atmosphere of our home. His dedication to a higher calling, while admirable, left a void in his family life—a void that he would come to regret deeply in his later years.

The Twilight of His Years

As the years passed, my grandfather's struggles became more pronounced. His spiritual practices, once a source of strength and clarity, began to take a toll on his well-being. In his latter days, he was a man plagued by regret and unhappiness. The peace of mind he had sought for so long remained beyond his reach, and the decisions he had made throughout his life began to weigh heavily on him.

It was clear that his inability to balance his spiritual aspirations with the demands of family life had left him feeling unfulfilled. He had sacrificed much in his pursuit of spiritual enlightenment, but what he gained in spiritual insights seemed to be offset by a deep sense of personal loss. He had neglected his relationships with those closest to him, and as a result, he faced his final days in a state of emotional and psychological distress.

My grandfather's story serves as a reminder of the complexity of human life and the challenges that come with striving for spiritual transcendence. While many admired him for his spiritual devotion, few understood the personal sacrifices he had made along the way. His lack of peace in his later years was a stark contrast to the image of a serene and enlightened ascetic that many had of him.

The Cost of Spiritual Pursuits

The life of my grandfather, Potana Lakshminarayana, offers a profound lesson about the importance of balance in life. His journey as a spiritual figure was undoubtedly inspiring to many, but it also serves as a cautionary tale about the dangers of neglecting one's personal and familial responsibilities in the pursuit of spiritual enlightenment. The disconnect between his spiritual aspirations and his responsibilities to his family left him in a state of deep regret during his final days. His inability to find peace of mind serves as a reminder that true fulfillment in life requires balance.

Spiritual pursuits are undoubtedly important, and the search for meaning beyond the material world is a journey that many undertake. However, as my grandfather's life shows, it is crucial to find a way to integrate these pursuits with the demands of everyday life. Neglecting one's family, friends, and responsibilities in the name of spiritual asceticism can lead to isolation, regret, and a lack of true peace. My grandfather's struggles with inner turmoil and lack of peace in his latter days are a testament to this truth.

As I reflect on my grandfather's life, I am reminded of the importance of seeking both spiritual and personal fulfillment. His life, though filled with spiritual depth, lacked the peace and meaning that come from nurturing relationships and fulfilling one's duties in the world. This is a lesson I carry with me, striving to honor both my spiritual journey and the responsibilities I have to those around me. In this way, I hope to find the balance that my grandfather struggled to achieve and, in doing so, honor his legacy while learning from his mistakes.

In the intricate tapestry of our lives, the threads of ancestry weave a profound narrative that often shapes our destiny in ways we scarcely understand. For me, the story begins with my maternal grandfather, Chinnam Rathaiah, whose life was a testament to unwavering faith and relentless perseverance. As a devoted Vaishnavite from Salempalem in Andhra Pradesh, his journey from hardship to prosperity was marked by both spiritual devotion and a deep-seated quest for peace. Despite his significant achievements and respected position in the community, the internal conflict between his disciplined religious practices and his search for inner tranquility reflects the complex interplay of faith and struggle that has influenced my own spiritual journey.

On the other side, the legacy of my paternal grandfather, Potana Lakshminarayana, a dedicated Shaivite, adds another layer to this rich ancestral narrative. His ascetic beliefs and the ensuing family conflicts with my maternal grandfather's Vaishnavite tradition not only highlight the religious dichotomies of our heritage but also set the stage for the challenges and transformations that would define my life. In understanding these ancestral roots, we unravel the foundational experiences that have shaped my own quest for spiritual truth and identity, leading to a deeper appreciation of the divine intervention that would later transform my path.

1.2 Maternal Vaishnavite Background

My maternal grandfather, **Chinnam Rathaiah**, was a devout follower of the Vaishnava tradition of Hinduism, dedicated to the worship of lord Vishnu. His entire life was centered

around his religious beliefs, and his unwavering devotion to Vishnu shaped not only his daily routines but also his moral values and his interactions with family and society. To him, the principles of dharma (righteousness) and devotion were not just abstract concepts but guiding forces that determined his actions.

Rathaiah's life as a Vaishnavite was deeply tied to the belief that devotion to lord Vishnu would ultimately lead to liberation from the cycle of birth and rebirth (samsara). He saw his worship and prayers as part of a larger cosmic plan, believing that by living a righteous life, he could attain moksha (spiritual liberation). Every morning and evening, he would engage in elaborate rituals—chanting mantras, offering food and flowers to the deity, and performing aarti (the waving of lamps). These rituals were essential to his sense of duty, his spiritual connection, and his identity as a devout Vaishnavite.

While Rathaiah was deeply connected to the divine, his religious devotion extended beyond personal worship. He was also committed to the Vaishnavite community and would actively participate in temple festivals, offer financial support to religious activities, and even encourage his family members to follow the path of devotion. His home was a place of sacredness, with an altar dedicated to Lord Vishnu, and visitors would often remark on the spiritual atmosphere that permeated the household.

However, while his religious life was

disciplined and his devotion was evident, the peace and contentment that he sought so fervently through his faith were always just beyond his grasp. Despite his unwavering belief in the power of devotion, Rathaiah struggled internally with feelings of unrest and dissatisfaction, which would haunt him throughout his life.

Early Struggles

Chinnam Rathaiah was born and raised in Salempalem, a small village nestled in the Krishna district of Andhra Pradesh, South India. The village, like many rural areas of India, was a place of stark contrasts—rich with natural beauty, but equally marked by economic hardship. The fields were lush with rice and different grains, the rivers were wide, and the monsoons brought much-needed rainfall to the agrarian landscape. Yet, for families like Rathaiah's, life was a continuous struggle against poverty and the uncertainty of subsistence farming.

Rathaiah's early life in Salempalem was filled with challenges. His family, like many others in the village, was poor and lived from one harvest to the next, constantly battling the vagaries of the weather and the limitations of a traditional rural economy. Food was often scarce, and access to education and healthcare was limited. Many of his peers were resigned to a life of poverty, following in the footsteps of their parents, with few opportunities for upward mobility.

But even as a young boy, Rathaiah was different. He was determined not to be confined by the circumstances of his birth. While his peers may have accepted their fate, Rathaiah had a vision for something greater. He saw education as his way out of poverty, and despite the financial challenges, he was committed to learning. His parents, though struggling to make ends meet, recognized his potential and supported his efforts, even when it meant making personal sacrifices. Rathaiah's early life in Salempalem instilled in him the values of hard work, perseverance, and resilience. These values would serve him well in the years to come as he embarked on a journey that would take him from the fields of Salempalem to the world of Ayurvedic medicine and, ultimately, to a position of respect and material prosperity in his community.

Education and Ayurvedic Medicine

Rathaiah's path to material prosperity was built on the foundation of education and his dedication to the ancient Indian practice of Ayurvedic medicine. Unlike many in his generation, Rathaiah had the rare opportunity to receive a formal education, which set him apart from others in his village. His intellectual curiosity and determination to improve his circumstances drove him to pursue his studies with an unwavering focus.

While many rural families saw education as an unattainable luxury, Rathaiah viewed it as his lifeline. He immersed himself in his studies, excelling in subjects that were often inaccessible to others in his community. Through sheer determination, he managed to gain admission to a formal institution where he could study Ayurveda, the traditional system of medicine that had been practiced in India for thousands of years.

Ayurveda, with its holistic approach to healing and its emphasis on balance between mind, body, and spirit, deeply resonated with Rathaiah's religious beliefs as a Vaishnavite. The principles of Ayurveda aligned with his understanding of the world—one in which health and well-being were intricately connected to the natural world and the divine. Through his studies, Rathaiah mastered the knowledge of herbal remedies, traditional therapies, and the Ayurvedic understanding of the body's *doshas* (biological energies). This expertise would form the cornerstone of his professional life.

After completing his studies, Rathaiah returned to his village with the knowledge and skills to practice Ayurveda. Word of his abilities quickly spread, and he soon became known as a trusted and skilled Ayurvedic doctor. People from nearby villages would come to him for treatment, seeking relief from a wide range of ailments—from chronic illnesses to minor injuries. Rathaiah's practice flourished, and as a result, he began to accumulate wealth and respect within the community.

Through his Ayurvedic practice, Rathaiah was not only able to provide for his family but also to transform his life. He had risen from the depths of poverty to a position of relative affluence. His hard work, dedication to his craft, and a deep sense of responsibility toward his patients had earned him a place of honor in his community.

A Family Man

While Chinnam Rathaiah's professional life was defined by his success as an Ayurvedic doctor, his personal life was centered around his large and bustling family. He was the proud father of two sons and seven daughters, and his home was always filled with the sounds of family life—children playing, grandchildren running through the halls, and family members gathering around for meals and conversations.

Raising such a large family was no small task, but Rathaiah embraced his role as a provider with great responsibility. His success in Ayurvedic medicine allowed him to support his children's education and ensure that they had opportunities he himself had struggled to attain. His two sons followed in his footsteps in their own way, both becoming government teachers. To Rathaiah, this was a source of immense pride, as he saw education as the key to breaking the cycle of poverty that had gripped his own family for generations.

Rathaiah's daughters, too, were well cared for. Though traditional societal norms often placed limitations on women's education and opportunities,

Rathaiah ensured that his daughters received the support and resources they needed to succeed in their own right. He believed that educating his daughters was just as important as educating his sons, and he worked tirelessly to ensure that they were well-prepared for their futures.

As the family grew, so did the number of grandchildren, and Rathaiah's home became a hub of activity. Family gatherings were frequent, and the house was always full of people. During holidays, festivals, and special occasions, the house would come alive with the sounds of celebration. Yet, even in the midst of such joy and familial closeness, there were moments of tension and struggle. While Rathaiah was a provider in the material sense, there were emotional and spiritual gaps that could not be filled by wealth or status.

Despite his efforts to create a prosperous and harmonious family life, Rathaiah often felt a sense of discontent. The peace he had hoped to cultivate within his family remained elusive, and the pressures of providing for such a large household weighed heavily on him. This inner conflict, though not always visible to others, would be a defining theme in his later years.

From Poverty to Landlord

Over the years, Chinnam Rathaiah's hard work and dedication to his Ayurvedic practice led to significant financial success. He used the wealth he accumulated from his practice to invest in land, eventually becoming a landlord in the region. In rural India, land ownership was not only a symbol of wealth but also of power and social status. By acquiring land, Rathaiah cemented his position as a prominent figure in the community, earning both respect and influence. As a landlord, Rathaiah was responsible for managing his property and the people who worked the land. This role brought with it a new set of challenges and responsibilities. In addition to his duties as a healer and family man, he was now also a landowner, tasked with ensuring that his land was productive and that those who worked for him were treated fairly.

His newfound status brought him considerable respect within the local society. People looked up to him not only as a doctor but also as a man of means and influence. His reputation for fairness and integrity further solidified his standing in the community, and he was often called upon to mediate disputes or provide guidance on important matters.

However, with this new position came the pressures of maintaining his wealth and status. The demands of managing land, combined with the responsibilities of his family and his religious devotion, began to weigh heavily on Rathaiah. While he had achieved material success, he had long sought peace and contentment.

Family Issues & Struggles

Chinnam Rathaiah's life was one of relentless hard work and dedication, both as a professional Ayurvedic doctor and as a family man. While his professional life brought him prosperity and respect in the community, his personal life was marked by a deep sense of turmoil, particularly when it came to the struggles his seven daughters faced in their married lives. As a father, Rathaiah had always taken pride in his large family, and he had worked tirelessly to provide for his seven daughters' well-being. However, the social and cultural expectations surrounding marriage in South India at the time brought immense challenges that he could not foresee.

In Indian society, daughters are traditionally seen as the responsibility of their fathers until they are married, at which point they are expected to become the responsibility of their husbands and in-laws. However, for Rathaiah's daughters, marriage did not always offer the security and stability that was expected. Many of his daughters faced significant family issues in their marital homes, ranging from financial pressures related to dowry to emotional and physical abuse. These problems were compounded by the societal expectations that women should endure such difficulties silently, without seeking divorce or separation, as marriages were considered sacred and permanent.

Rathaiah's daughters often found themselves in difficult situations, where they were expected to conform to the demands of their husbands and in-laws, sometimes at great personal cost. As a father, Rathaiah felt a profound sense of responsibility for his daughters' well-being, and witnessing their suffering caused him immense emotional pain. He had provided for them, educated them, and married them into what he believed were suitable families, but he was powerless to prevent the hardships they faced in their married lives.

Dowry and Marital Problems

One of the most significant issues that plagued Rathaiah's daughters' marriages was the cultural practice of dowry. In South India, as in many parts of the country, the dowry system—where the bride's family provides money, goods, or property to the groom's family as part of the marriage arrangement—was deeply entrenched. Although Rathaiah had managed to accumulate wealth through his Ayurvedic practice and landownership, the financial strain of marrying off seven daughters with significant dowries was immense.

Beyond the financial burden, the dowry system also created a power dynamic within marriages that often left women vulnerable to mistreatment. Rathaiah's daughters were no exception. Several of them faced harassment and pressure from their in-laws, who demanded more dowry even after the marriages had taken place. This led to ongoing conflicts within their marital homes, where they were often blamed for failing to bring enough wealth into the family.

Divorce, in those days, was not seen as a viable option due to the strict religious and cultural norms that governed marriage in Vaishnavite and Hindu traditions. Marriages were considered sacred and unbreakable, and divorce was highly discouraged, if not outright stigmatized. The social pressure to maintain the sanctity of marriage, even in the face of severe difficulties, meant that Rathaiah's daughters were expected to endure their suffering in silence. This left them trapped in marriages that were emotionally and, in some cases, physically abusive.

For Rathaiah, this was a source of deep anguish. As a deeply religious man, he upheld the values of commitment and duty, believing that marriage was a divine bond that should be honored. Yet, seeing his daughters suffer under the weight of these same societal and religious expectations caused him great inner conflict. He found himself torn between his adherence to religious tradition and his desire to protect his daughters from harm.

A Father's Responsibility

As the family issues in their marriages became too difficult to bear, several of Rathaiah's daughters made the painful decision to return to their parental home, often with their children in tow. This was not an uncommon practice in India, where women who faced marital strife would seek refuge in their father's home. However, for Rathaiah, this meant taking on the additional burden of providing for not only his daughters but also his grandchildren.

The return of his daughters to his home placed enormous financial and emotional pressure on Rathaiah. His home, which had once been filled with the joy of raising his children and the prosperity of his successful medical practice, now became a refuge for daughters who had been wounded by their marital experiences. The house, already full of people, now had to accommodate additional members, and Rathaiah had to shoulder the responsibility of providing for their needs.

Beyond the financial strain, Rathaiah also had to contend with the emotional toll that these family issues took on him. Seeing his daughters return home, often broken and dispirited, filled him with a profound sense of helplessness. As a father, he had always believed that it was his duty to ensure their happiness and well-being, but the harsh realities of their marriages shattered this belief. He found himself grappling with feelings of guilt and sorrow, questioning whether he had done enough to protect them from the societal pressures that had led to their suffering.

Despite these challenges, Rathaiah never turned his back on his daughters. He provided for them to the best of his ability, offering them and their children a place of safety and support. However, the weight of these family struggles left a lasting impact on him, one that would shape the remainder of his life.

The Search for Peace Through Religion

Throughout his life, Chinnam Rathaiah remained a deeply devout Vaishnavite, placing his faith in the worship of Lord Vishnu and the practice of religious rituals. He believed that his devotion would bring peace and stability not only to his own life but also to the lives of his family members. Every day, he performed his personal pujas and chanted sacred mantras, seeking divine intervention and protection for his family.

However, as the years passed and the struggles

with his daughters' marital issues continued, Rathaiah began to experience a growing sense of restlessness. Despite his unwavering faith and his disciplined religious practices, the peace he sought through devotion seemed increasingly out of reach. His daughters' suffering, the financial strain of supporting their return to his home, and the emotional toll of witnessing their hardships left him feeling disillusioned.

Rathaiah's religious devotion, which had once been a source of strength and comfort, now seemed inadequate in the face of the complex challenges he faced. He continued to perform his daily rituals, but the sense of fulfillment and spiritual contentment he had hoped to achieve remained elusive. The family struggles had created a deep sense of turmoil within him, and no matter how devoutly he prayed or how strictly he adhered to religious observances, the peace he longed for never materialized.

In the end, Rathaiah's life was a poignant reminder of the limitations of religious devotion when faced with the harsh realities of life. His personal journey was one of inner conflict and a constant search for peace that he could never quite find in his Vaishnavite tradition. His struggles with his daughters' family issues, coupled with the societal pressures that dictated their lives, left him grappling with the complexities of duty, devotion, and the pursuit of happiness.

Though he remained a devout Vaishnavite until the end of his life, maternal grandfather's story is one of both devotion and disillusionment—a man who, despite his best efforts, was never able to reconcile the ideals of his faith with the realities of the world around him.

1.3 Family Conflicts and Religious Divide

As discussed earlier, in traditional Hinduism, Shaivism and Vaishnavism represent two major sects. These differing beliefs, though part of the same religious framework, have often sparked tension between followers of the two sects. In our family, these religious distinctions created a deep-seated conflict, shaping generations of interactions and leading to enmity between my paternal and maternal families.

These differences may have seemed small from an outside perspective, but within our families, they represented significant ideological and religious divides. These two strong-willed men, each entrenched in their respective beliefs, became symbols of the broader conflict between Shaivism and Vaishnavism. Their disagreements over religious practices extended beyond personal faith and led to familial discord. Over time, these differences fueled a deeper enmity, affecting not only them but also the relationship between their children and grandchildren.

Influence of Shaivite Asceticism

My father, Potana Nancharaiah, grew up under the strong influence of his father's Shaivite beliefs. From an early age, he was exposed to the ascetic life that my grandfather embraced, one that prioritized detachment from material concerns, focusing instead on spiritual purity and austerity. As a young man, my father was on a promising career path, working in Hyderabad and establishing a life for our family. However, his internal struggle with his identity as a Shaivite eventually took over.

When I was just two years old, my father made the fateful decision to leave his job, his responsibilities, and our family. He had become captivated by the ascetic lifestyle, choosing to pursue spiritual enlightenment over worldly concerns. At the time, my elder brother was four, and I was still a baby. The decision to leave us behind caused deep pain and suffering for my mother, who was suddenly thrust into the position of raising two young children on her own.

Hyderabad, a bustling city filled with opportunities, represented a path my father could have followed to secure our future. Instead, his departure marked the beginning of a series of challenges for our family. His decision was not just a personal one but was deeply connected to the religious conflict between the Shaivite and Vaishnavite traditions that ran through our family history.

The Move to Salempalem: My Mother's Struggle

After my father abandoned us, my mother, a resilient woman, made the difficult decision to return to her maternal home in Salempalem. She took my brother and me with her, hoping to find solace and support from her father and mother. My mother's suffering was immense. She had to come to terms with the betrayal of her husband and the heavy burden of caring for two young children without any means of financial stability.

Salempalem was a small village in the Krishna district of Andhra Pradesh, where my maternal grandfather, Chinna Rathaiah, had established himself as a respected Ayurvedic doctor and landlord. My grandmother, a nurturing presence in the home, provided much-needed comfort to my mother, but the emotional and psychological toll on her was evident. My mother's daily life revolved around the struggle to maintain a sense of normalcy for us, even as she carried the weight of abandonment and societal judgment.

As children, my brother and I were too young to fully understand the gravity of what had happened, but the emotional tension in the house was palpable. My mother's pain became a constant undercurrent in our lives, and her endurance during this period is something I came to appreciate only later.

2. My Birth and Divine Care

I was born on August 20, 1974, in the serene village of Salempalem, nestled in the Krishna district of Andhra Pradesh, South India. Salempalem is a picturesque village nestled on the serene shores of the Krishna River, embodying a harmonious blend of natural beauty and deep-rooted spirituality. The village is renowned for its lush, fertile paddy fields, which stretch out in verdant patches, shimmering with the promise of abundant harvests. These fields are nurtured by the life-giving waters of the Krishna River, which meanders gently, adding to the village's tranquil charm.

Since Hindu spirituality is the center of village life, one may feel the spiritual soul of the community. The air is often filled with the soft strains of devotional music and the fragrant aroma of incense from the temples that dot the landscape. These temples, often adorned with intricate carvings and vibrant murals, serve as focal points for the community's religious practices and festivals. The villagers, deeply devoted, celebrate various Hindu rituals and festivals with great enthusiasm, creating a rich tapestry of cultural and spiritual traditions.

The people of the village are known for their warmth and hospitality. There's a palpable sense of love and affection among the villagers, who are always ready to welcome visitors with open arms and genuine smiles. Community ties are strong, with neighbors supporting each other in times of need and coming together to celebrate joyous occasions. This sense of togetherness is evident in the way they share their harvests, participate in communal activities, and uphold the values of respect and kindness. I entered the world in a nurturing and intellectually stimulating environment, born to **Potana Nancharaiah and Manikyala Devi**. My father, Potana Nancharaiah, was a well-educated mechanical engineer who had

established a successful career in Hyderabad, embodying both professional excellence and a commitment to continuous learning. My mother, Manikyala Devi, was a devoted housewife whose life was deeply rooted in spirituality, dedicating herself to the spiritual and emotional well-being of the family.

2.1 Miraculous Preservation

Life has often felt like a tapestry woven with threads of miraculous events, each one affirming the belief that divine protection has been a constant in my journey. Reflecting on my early years reveals a series of close calls with death that seem to speak of a higher power guiding and safeguarding me. My mother's stories and my brother's acts of bravery underscore a life preserved by extraordinary means.

The Grueling Journey

In the days of my infancy, when transport facilities were non-existent, the journey from Machilipatnam to Salempalem was a grueling endeavor. My family, enduring the hardships of rural life, had to make the trip on foot. The distance was formidable, and the journey took hours, often through harsh conditions with no other means of conveyance. My mother, accompanied by relatives, embarked on this arduous trek, carrying me, a mere three-month-old baby, in her arms.

The journey was not only physically taxing but also fraught with uncertainties. There were no reliable roads or paths, and the landscape was largely uncharted. The travelers had to rely on their endurance and resourcefulness to navigate through vast stretches of land. Despite the grueling conditions, their determination to reach Salempalem, where hope and solace awaited, kept them moving forward.

A Life-Threatening Crisis

During this arduous journey, my mother experienced a crisis that would become a poignant chapter in our family's history. I had succumbed to a severe fever, and my condition worsened to the point where I was no longer responsive. In her arms, I was lifeless, showing no movement or signs of life. My mother's anguish was palpable as she faced the terrifying prospect of losing her infant child in the midst of this challenging journey.

The fever had taken a toll on me, and the situation seemed dire. My mother, already weary from the long trek and the oppressive heat, was now confronted with the prospect of losing me. The sense of helplessness was overwhelming, and her desperation was matched only by her resolve to save me.

A Search for Help

The journey took a darker turn as they found themselves in a remote area, far from any villages or human settlements. The isolation was complete; there were no nearby homes or towns where help could be sought. The lack of access to medical care or even basic assistance exacerbated the crisis. In the face of this profound isolation, my mother and relatives were left with limited options. They had no access to medical supplies or expert guidance, and the journey's hardships had taken their toll on their spirits. Despite the odds, my mother's faith and resolve did not waver.

The Power of Faith and Tradition

In her desperation, my mother recalled an old remedy recommended by her father, who was an Ayurvedic doctor. The remedy involved squeezing an onion into my nostrils. This practice, though unconventional, was rooted in her father's medical knowledge and traditional wisdom.

With no other alternatives available, my mother decided to try this remedy. Holding onto hope and faith, she applied the onion remedy as best as she could under the circumstances. Miraculously, I sneezed, and this small yet profound act of revival signaled a glimmer of hope. The remedy seemed to restore life to my frail body, marking a pivotal moment in the journey. This incident not only saved my life but also strengthened my mother's belief in the power of traditional remedies and divine intervention.

2.2 The Role of My Brother

As I grew older, my life continued to be a series of near-death experiences, each one underscoring the protective hand of a higher power. My brother, who was a few years older than me, played a crucial role in saving my life on several occasions. One notable incident involved a near-drowning experience in a canal.

The canal waters were deep and treacherous, and I fell in during play. My brother, demonstrating remarkable courage and quick thinking, jumped into the canal to rescue me. He managed to pull me out of the water and bring me to safety. This was not an isolated incident; my brother's bravery was a recurring theme in my life, with him saving me from various dangerous situations. His acts of heroism and quick thinking were instrumental in preserving my life, and they stand as a testament to the protective forces at work.

2.3 Realization of a Divine Plan

Reflecting on these miraculous moments, I am struck by the realization that my life has been guided by a divine plan. The series of near-death experiences, coupled with the miraculous interventions that preserved me, suggest that there is a higher purpose behind my existence. These experiences have not only shaped my belief in divine protection but have also deepened my understanding of the providence and guidance that have been part of my life.

The repeated instances of survival against the odds reveal a pattern of protection and intervention that cannot be explained by chance alone. Each close call with death and subsequent miraculous recovery underscores the belief that my life has been safeguarded for a purpose beyond my comprehension.

A Testimony to Divine Protection

As you delve into my story, the recurring theme of divine intervention and protection becomes evident. My life has been a series of miraculous events that highlight the sovereign protection, provision, and preparation that have been present throughout my journey. From the fever of my infancy to the acts of bravery by my brother, each chapter of my life serves as a testament to the divine forces that have guided and protected me.

These experiences have instilled in me a deep sense of gratitude and reverence for the divine presence that has been a constant in my life. They remind me of the importance of recognizing and appreciating the miracles that have shaped my existence and continue to guide me.

In the grand narrative of my life, these threads of divine intervention weave a story of protection, guidance, and purpose. They serve as a reminder of the benevolent forces at work and the profound impact they have had on my journey.

3. Pain and Perseverance

For my mother, life became a daily battle. She had to navigate not only the societal pressures of being a single mother in a traditional village but also the internal conflict between the Shaivite and Vaishnavite traditions. She had been raised in a devout Vaishnavite home, and now, through her marriage, she was connected to a Shaivite family. This religious tension added another layer of complexity to her struggle.

Her devotion to us, her children, never wavered. Even in the face of adversity, she found the strength to provide for us and ensure that we received an education. She sought help from her brothers, who became instrumental in our upbringing. My mother's pain was not just physical but emotional, as she had to endure the scorn of society, the absence of her husband, and the burden of raising two children alone.

3.1 Father's Absence and Maternal Support

During this challenging time, my mother's elder brothers, Lakshmana Swamy, and Venugopala Swamy, stepped in to support us. They became father figures in my life, offering the guidance and care that my own father had forsaken. Without their unwavering support, our lives could have taken a much darker turn.

Lakshmana Swamy and Venugopala Swamy were both well-respected individuals within the community. They helped my mother financially, emotionally, and spiritually. My uncle Venugopala Swamy, in particular, took a personal interest in my well-being. He helped me get admission into a boarding school, which was a turning point in my life.

This act of kindness gave me the opportunity to focus on my studies, even though I was separated from my family during those formative years.

3.2 Childhood Labor and Responsibilities

I was a small boy in the 5th grade when my mother made the difficult decision to leave me at my uncle Lakshmana Swamy's home in Salempalem. It was a moment that marked a significant turning point in my life, separating me from my mother and brother. At such a young age, I didn't fully grasp the weight of the situation, but I quickly realized that life would be different.

My uncle Lakshmana Swamy, though kind, had a household to manage, and my position there was one of both family and labor. I was dependent on him and his family for shelter, food, and care, but in return, I had to shoulder responsibilities that would shape my understanding of hard work and perseverance. I was no longer a child in the traditional sense; I had become part of the household workforce.

Life at my uncle's home was tough, and every day began before sunrise. The household depended on my contributions to keep things running smoothly, and

I was determined to prove myself useful, even though the tasks assigned to me were arduous for a child my age.

Daily Labor: Early Mornings and Heavy Responsibilities

My mornings started earlier than most. Before the village awoke, I had to begin my chores. One of my primary tasks was cleaning the buffalo shed. This was not just a simple task of tidying up; the shed was filled with dung and filth accumulated overnight, and it had to be cleaned before 6 am. I would wake up before dawn and make my way to the shed, where the pungent smell of buffalo dung greeted me. Armed with only basic tools, I cleaned the area, scraping away the mess and ensuring it was spotless for the day ahead.

The physical labor was intense for a boy of my age, but there was no option to complain. I had to prove myself worthy of the roof over my head. The sense of responsibility weighed heavily on me, and the task had to be completed before the rest of the household stirred awake. There was no running water in the village, so once I finished with the buffalo shed, I had to walk to the nearby pond to fetch water for the household.

The pond was the lifeline of the village, as there

were no taps or pipelines to provide water. Every family depended on the pond for their daily needs. I would carry a pot, often too heavy for my small frame, and walk to the pond, fill it, and bring it back to the house. The journey back was slow and tiring, as the water pot on my head added weight to my already exhausted body. This was my daily routine—one that continued day after day.

Collecting Firewood: The Struggle for Basic Necessities

In the village, firewood was the primary source of fuel for cooking. Unlike modern households that rely on gas stoves, the people of Salempalem depended on wood to cook their meals. One of my responsibilities was to gather firewood for the household. This task was especially difficult because the trees where we sourced the wood were not close by, and carrying the heavy load back home was physically demanding.

I would set out into the fields and woods with a small axe, searching for dry branches and fallen trees. The process of cutting and gathering enough wood to sustain the household's cooking needs was both time-consuming and exhausting. Once I had gathered a sufficient amount, I would carry the load back to the house, often with my arms and back aching from the effort. This was a task I had to complete regularly, as cooking was a daily necessity, and the firewood supply had to be constantly replenished.

Despite the physical toll, I took pride in my work. I understood that without my efforts, the household wouldn't function as smoothly, and this gave me a sense of purpose, even in the midst of hardship.

No Shoes and Self-Reliance: A Lesson in Resilience

Another aspect of my life at my uncle's home was the need for self-reliance. Unlike many children my age, I had to wash my clothes. There was no one to do this for me, and the lack of basic amenities meant that I had to make do with limited resources. Washing clothes by hand, fetching water, and managing my own needs became a routine part of my life.

What made this even more challenging was the fact that I had never owned a pair of shoes. From my early childhood, until I entered college at the age of 19, I walked barefoot everywhere. Whether I was at school, at home, or out in the fields collecting firewood, I did so without any footwear. The rough terrain of the village often left my feet bruised and sore, but it became a normal part of my life. I didn't think much of it at the time, but looking back, I realize how much resilience it built in me. The lack of shoes was a symbol of the poverty and struggles we faced, but it also became a source of strength. I learned to endure, to push through discomfort, and to survive in challenging circumstances.

3.3 Moments of Accident and Divine Care

One of the most vivid memories from this period of my life was a particular day when I was tasked with fetching water, as usual. Every family member had their pot, and mine was a special brass pot, heavy and durable. This pot was precious, and I was responsible for filling it each day. One afternoon, after a long day of chores, I went to the pond to fetch water. The pot, once filled, became significantly heavier, and as I attempted to lift it onto my head, my grip slipped.

The brass pot, now full of water, fell from my hands and crashed onto the cement steps of the pond, landing squarely on my left little finger. The pain was immediate and excruciating. I fell to the ground, clutching my hand, as blood began to pool around my smashed finger. The impact had been so severe that my finger was crushed against the cement step.

There was no one around to help me, and for a moment, I felt an overwhelming sense of fear. The pond, deep and quiet, loomed beside me, and I realized how easily I could have slipped into the water and drowned. But in that moment of desperation, something miraculous happened. Though I didn't know God at the time, I now believe that it was His mercy that saved me. Somehow, despite the severity of the injury, I managed to stand up, gather myself, and make my way back home. My little finger was severely wounded, and the scar remains to this day as a reminder of that moment.

The incident left a deep impression on me. It was a turning point in my understanding of life's fragility and the unseen hand of divine protection. Though I was a small boy with no knowledge of God, I survived that day, and it was an experience that would shape my spiritual journey in the years to come.

Life at my uncle's home in Salempalem was marked by hardship, responsibility, and physical labor, but it also taught me valuable lessons in resilience, endurance, and faith. The tasks I had to complete—cleaning the buffalo shed, fetching water, gathering firewood, and enduring the pain of going without shoes—were all part of a larger journey. These experiences, though difficult, shaped me into a person who could withstand adversity and find strength in the midst of struggle.

The accident with the brass pot and the scar that remains on my finger are reminders of both the physical and spiritual challenges I faced during those years. Even when I didn't understand the workings of divine intervention, I was being protected and guided through the trials of my young life. These early experiences laid the foundation for the faith and perseverance that would carry me through the rest of my life.

Though I worked hard and contributed to my uncle Lakshmana Swamy's household by helping with various domestic chores, it became clear that he saw me as a burden for the future. Despite my best efforts, he was not willing to keep mc in his home any longer. This rejection deeply affected me, but amidst the uncertainty, my grandmother, who had always been a source of comfort and love, stepped in. She took it upon herself to find a solution and decided to take me to my other uncle, Venugopala Swamy, who lived in Koduru town.

This marked the beginning of a new chapter in my life. Venugopala Swamy welcomed me into his home, and life in Koduru offered new opportunities and experiences. Though the past had been filled with hardship, this move felt like a fresh start, opening the door to growth and learning in a new environment. It was here, under the care of my uncle, that I would continue my journey, finding strength in the challenges and hope in the changes ahead.

3.4 New Life Begins

Arriving at my uncle Venugopala Swamy's home was like stepping into a world of care and affection that I had not fully experienced before. His wife, Mrs. Rangamma, who was my cousin (my mother's sister's daughter), treated me with warmth

and motherly love. She made sure I had good food and took care of my needs as if I were her child. This environment felt like a relief after the struggles I had faced in my earlier years at Salempalem. At Venugopala Swamy's house, I found a sense of belonging that helped me heal from the emotional and physical hardships I had endured.

The love and care I received in this home

became a source of great comfort and strength for me. Though my life had been difficult up until this point, I now felt a sense of security and support. My aunt, with her nurturing nature, provided not just food but also emotional nourishment. Her kindness and attentiveness made me feel valued in a way I hadn't before, and for the first time in a long while, I began to experience the joys of childhood again.

3.4.1 Sweet Memories with My Cousins

Living at my uncle Venugopala Swamy's home also brought me closer to my cousins, Leela Krishna, Srikrishna, and Bhuvanakrishna. These relationships were vital to my well-being, as they offered me the companionship I had longed for. Among them, Leela Krishna was closest to me in age, and naturally, we bonded as playmates. We spent hours together, creating memories that I cherish to this day. Whether it was playing in the fields or running around the house, our laughter filled the air, giving me a sense of joy that was absent from my life before.

Leela Krishna and I shared a special connection, being of the same age and growing up together. Our bond helped me cope with the difficulties of my past as we played and studied together. He became not only a cousin but a true friend, someone who could understand the challenges of childhood and offer companionship in moments of loneliness. Our games and conversations brought light into my life, reminding me that there was still room for happiness even amidst all the struggles.

Srikrishna and Bhuvanakrishna, though older, also played important roles in my life. I admired their maturity and their willingness to help out when needed. They were like older brothers, guiding me through the complexities of growing up in a household that valued family bonds and responsibility. Each of them contributed to shaping my experiences, making my time in their home full of love, support, and shared moments that I will always remember.

A Selfless Act of Kindness

Of all my cousins, Bhuvanakrishna stood out for his generosity and willingness to help me when I needed it the most. I will always be deeply grateful to him for his efforts in helping me secure a hostel seat in a government boarding school. This was a complex task. It required navigating the complex bureaucracy of government offices, dealing with officials, and ensuring that all the paperwork was in order. Bhuvanakrishna took it upon himself to handle these challenges for me.

Thanks to his selfless dedication, I was able to get a hostel seat in a government boarding school that provided free shelter and education. This was a life-changing opportunity for me. The school became my sanctuary from the difficulties of home life, offering me a structured environment where I could focus on my studies and personal growth. The school provided me with not just an education but a stable home from the 6th grade to the 10th grade, giving me the chance to grow academically and socially in ways I hadn't imagined before.

I often think about how different my life could have been if Bhuvanakrishna had not stepped in to help. Without the shelter and education provided by the hostel, my future might have been bleak, and my dreams of completing school could have been cut short. Bhuvanakrishna's kindness and willingness to go out of his way to help me are things I will never forget, and I remain deeply grateful to him for opening the door to new opportunities and a brighter future.

3.4.2 Life in the Government Boarding School

Life in the government boarding school was an experience unlike any other. The challenges were relentless, and the conditions were far from ideal, but these hardships also helped shape my character and perseverance. The moment I entered the school, it became clear that survival was as much a part of my education as the subjects I was studying. Every day, I presented a new obstacle, testing my will and determination to keep moving forward.

The environment was harsh and unforgiving. The facilities were minimal, and the lack of necessities made it difficult to focus on academics. Still, I was grateful to have a place to stay and the opportunity for an education, even if it came at such a high personal cost. There was no luxury or comfort here, only the daily grind of getting through each day with whatever resources we could muster. I quickly learned that I would have to depend on my resilience and inner strength to get by.

The conditions in the boarding school made me appreciate the smallest of things. Basic needs like food, shelter, and electricity were never guaranteed, and it was often a struggle to make it through the day. Despite the difficulties, I committed myself to remain focused on my education. No matter how tough things got, I knew that this was my only chance to change my future, and I couldn't afford to give up.

Studying in the Dark

One of the most difficult challenges I faced at the boarding school was the frequent lack of electricity. Without proper lighting, studying became almost impossible, and the nights were especially challenging. We had to rely on kerosene lamps to provide some light, but even that came with its own set of problems. The

dim glow of the kerosene lamp was hardly sufficient for reading or writing, and the fumes from the burning kerosene often filled the room, making it hard to breathe.

On many occasions, I didn't even have money to buy kerosene, which left me with no choice but to study in near darkness. I would squint at my books, trying to make out the words in the faint light, determined not to let the lack of resources stop me from learning. Those were some of the hardest nights, but they were also the moments that taught me the value of perseverance.

The lack of electricity wasn't just an inconvenience; it was a constant reminder of how little we had. Yet, despite these difficulties, I refused to let the circumstances defeat me. I saw education as my only way out of this life, and I was determined to make the most of the opportunity, no matter how dim the light was.

The Harsh Reality of School Life

The boarding school wasn't just tough because of the poor facilities—it was also a place where the students had to deal with each other's aggression and frustrations. With so many children crammed into the same space, fights were common, and tempers often flared. It was a rough environment where survival of the fittest seemed to be the unspoken rule.

The children came from different backgrounds, many of them having experienced hardship in their own lives, which made them tough and, at times, aggressive. There was a constant sense of competition, and conflicts could break out over the smallest things— a stolen pencil, a dirty look, or simply being in the wrong place at the wrong time. It wasn't uncommon for arguments to turn into physical altercations, and I had to be on guard at all times.

The rough lifestyle extended beyond the fights. The lack of supervision and structure in the hostel meant that many of the children developed bad habits and indulged in behaviors that weren't conducive to learning. I had to navigate this chaotic environment carefully, avoiding trouble while staying focused on my studies. It wasn't easy, but I made it my mission to rise above the conflicts and distractions, keeping my eye on the ultimate goal: a better future through education.

Contagious Diseases and Poor Living Conditions

Another constant challenge at the boarding

school was the widespread presence of contagious skin diseases. With so many children living in close quarters and poor hygiene standards, infections spread quickly. Skin rashes, boils, and other ailments were common, and it was almost impossible to avoid them.

The living conditions contributed to this problem. There was little access to clean water, and the shared bathrooms and sleeping areas were breeding grounds for germs. We had to share everything—mats, clotheslines, even the same bowls and plates—which made it easy for diseases to spread from one student to another. There was little medical care available, so most of us just had to suffer through the infections and hope that they would eventually go away.

Despite the discomfort and the threat of illness, I tried my best to maintain my focus. I knew that these were just more obstacles to overcome and that I couldn't let them distract me from my studies. While many of the other children gave in to the rough lifestyle, I made a conscious decision to stay disciplined and not let my environment pull me down.

Spoiled Food and Survival

The food served at the hostel was another major

challenge. Most of the time, the rice was spoiled, and the meals were barely edible. In the afternoons, we were given a small portion of curry, but it was never enough to satisfy our hunger. The worst was in the evenings when all we had to eat was tamarind water, commonly known as "*rasam*." It was a thin, watery broth that provided no real nutrition, and even worse, the rice often had small white worms floating in it.

I still remember the sight of those worms on my plate, wriggling among the grains of rice. At first, the sight disgusted me, and I would try to remove the worms before eating. But over time, I became so accustomed to it that I ate the rice, worms and all. It wasn't a matter of choice anymore—it was survival. The food was all we had, and there was no alternative. Eating the rice, no matter how spoiled it was, became part of the daily routine.

The poor quality of the food didn't matter to me as much as my education. I learned to accept the circumstances and focused on what I could control: my studies. While others complained and grew frustrated, I kept my attention on my books. I knew that this was a temporary situation and that education was my ticket out of this life.

The Power of Focus

Despite all the hardships—the lack of electricity, the fights, the diseases, and the spoiled food—I never let myself lose sight of why I was there. Education was my only hope, and I clung to it with everything I had. The conditions in the boarding school may have been terrible, but I knew that the knowledge I was gaining would eventually open doors to a better life.

Every challenge I faced only strengthened my resolve. I told myself that if I could survive the boarding school, I could survive anything. I stayed focused on my studies, spending every spare moment reading and learning, even when the kerosene lamp barely gave enough light or when my stomach ached from hunger. My circumstances may have been dire, but I refused to let them dictate my future.

In the end, the hardships I faced at the boarding school became a testament to my determination. It wasn't easy, but I emerged stronger, more resilient, and more committed to achieving my dreams. Through it all, I never lost sight of the importance of education, and that focus would carry me through the rest of my life.

3.4.3 Weekends and Holidays: A Homely Escape

Though I spent most of my time at the government boarding school, weekends and holidays were my chance to return to my uncle Venugopala Swamy's home, where I was always welcomed with open arms. These moments became precious to me as they gave me the chance to experience a warm, homely environment. After the structured life of the hostel, being able to come back to my uncle's house felt like a return to love and care.

During these weekends, I would relish the simple pleasures that I had once taken for granted: home-cooked meals, conversations with family, and the feeling of being in a place where I belonged. The food, in particular, was something I looked forward to, as it was a welcome change from the more basic meals provided by the hostel. My aunt always made sure I was well-fed, preparing dishes that nourished both my body and soul. This nurturing care from her became one of the most comforting aspects of my life at the time.

The time I spent with my cousins during these breaks, I was also continued to be a source of joy. Playing with Leela Krishna, chatting with Srikrishna and Bhuvanakrishna, and being part of family gatherings allowed me to experience a sense of normalcy that had been missing from my early childhood. These visits home, though brief, were rejuvenating and gave me the strength I needed to continue my studies and responsibilities at the hostel.

A New Chapter of Growth and Belonging

Looking back, my time at my uncle Venugopala Swamy's home marked a significant period of growth in my life. It was during these years that I began to transition from a boy burdened by hardship to a young person filled with hope for the future. The love and care I received from my uncle, his wife, and my cousins helped me regain my confidence and sense of self-worth. The stability and nurturing environment they provided allowed me to focus on my education and personal development.

The contrast between my early years of hardship and the support I received at Venugopala Swamy's home couldn't have been more striking. It was here that I learned the importance of family bonds and how acts of kindness and care can transform a life. My uncle and his family didn't just provide me with a roof over my head; they gave me the emotional support I needed to overcome the challenges of my past and prepare for a brighter future.

As I moved forward in life, these formative years became the foundation upon which I built my resilience, my gratitude, and my determination to succeed. The love I received, the memories I made, and the support I was given at my uncle's home will forever remain a cherished part of my life's journey.

3.4.4 Venugopala Swamy's Role

From 6th grade until I completed 10th grade, my uncle Venugopala Swamy played a critical role in ensuring I had the necessary resources to succeed. The decision to send me to a boarding school was not an easy one, but it was necessary. At school, I found myself isolated from my family, which was emotionally challenging. However, my uncle's visits, his words of encouragement, and his financial support helped me push through the difficulties.

Boarding school became a place of refuge but

also a source of intense longing for familial warmth. I often cried at night, yearning for my mother, father, and brother. The emotional toll of living away from home made me develop a deep spiritual yearning for divine help.

3.4.5 Lakshmana Swamy's Role

While Venugopala Swamy took care of my needs, my other uncle, Lakshmana Swamy, helped my elder brother, Srinivasa Rao. He ensured that my brother received the support and care he needed, especially as he navigated his journey through school and adolescence. Both of my uncles played pivotal roles in keeping our scattered family afloat, as my brother and I were separated from each other and our parents due to the circumstances created by my father's decisions.

The bond between my brother and me remained strong despite the physical distance between us. We shared a common understanding of the pain caused by our father's abandonment and found comfort in knowing that our uncles were there for us.

Spiritual Struggles and Longing for Divine Help

As a child, my experiences in boarding school

and the absence of my father created a deep spiritual yearning within me. I often found myself crying out to God, asking for His divine intervention. My desire to experience God's presence grew with each passing day, and I longed for spiritual guidance in a world that seemed overwhelmingly difficult. The trials and struggles of my early years forged in me a strong desire to seek out God's blessings, to understand His plan for my life, and to find peace in His presence.

I prayed fervently, hoping that God would reveal Himself to me and provide the strength I needed to overcome the pain of separation and abandonment. This spiritual longing became a central part of my identity, shaping my relationship with God in profound ways.

Academic Achievement: Triumph Amidst Struggle

Despite the emotional and spiritual challenges, I faced, I was determined to succeed academically. My experiences at boarding school, though difficult, taught me the value of perseverance and hard work. By the time I reached the 10th grade, I had developed a strong work ethic fueled by my desire to make something of myself despite the hardships I had endured.

When I completed my 10th grade in Koduru town, Krishna district, I achieved the first rank in my school. This accomplishment was a testament to my resilience and determination. It was not just a personal victory but a moment of triumph for my entire family, particularly for my mother, who had sacrificed so much to ensure that I received an education.

A Journey of Struggle, Faith, and Triumph

Looking back, the conflicts between Shaivism and Vaishnavism in our family set the stage for a life filled with challenges. My father's departure, influenced by his Shaivite asceticism, created a ripple effect that affected every aspect of our lives. My mother's strength, the unwavering support of my uncles, and my spiritual journey were all integral parts of my story. Despite the struggles, I emerged stronger, with a deep sense of faith and a desire to continue seeking God's guidance.

3.5 A Glimmer of Hope

At a pivotal moment in my life, things seemed to be improving. My father, after many years of embracing an ascetic lifestyle in the forest, finally realized his mistake. He returned to Salempalem, bringing with him the hope that our family could begin to heal from the hardships caused by his long absence. His return brought a sense of reconciliation and a chance to rebuild what had been lost. For the first time in many years, I felt that things were looking up.

I had just completed my 10th-grade studies with flying colors, earning the first rank in my school. I had worked hard, believing that education was my way out of the poverty and suffering that had defined my childhood. With my father back in the picture, I was hopeful that he and my mother would now be able to support me as I pursued higher education. For the first time, the future seemed promising, and I allowed myself to dream of a college education that would change the course of my life.

However, beneath that initial hope, reality soon set in. While my father's return was a blessing in many ways, it quickly became clear that the years he had spent in the forest had taken a toll on his ability to provide for us.

A Harsh Reality: My Father's Struggles

Despite my father's return, our family's financial situation remained dire. My father, who had once been an educated man with potential, had lost much of his ability to secure meaningful employment. Years of ascetic living had aged him prematurely, and the opportunities for a man of his age and background were scarce. Unable to find a stable job, he resorted to working as a daily wage laborer, toiling in the agricultural fields of our village.

Watching my father, who had once been a source of strength and intelligence, reduced to the role of a coolie was heartbreaking. I could see the frustration and sadness in his eyes as he struggled to provide for our family. Despite his best efforts, he was no longer able to offer the kind of financial support that was needed for my education. The reality of our situation became painfully clear: I was on my own if I wanted to continue my studies.

This realization was devastating. I had done everything in my power to excel academically, believing that if I worked hard enough, I would find a way to pursue higher education. But now, with no resources and no financial backing, my dreams seemed to be slipping away.

3.5.3 Crying Out to the gods: A Desperate Search

As my dreams of attending college began to crumble, I turned to the only source of hope I knew: the Hindu gods. I had grown up in a devout family, and from a young age, I had been taught that the gods had the power to intervene in the lives of their devotees. I prayed fervently, visiting temples and offering my prayers to the gods. I begged for a miracle, hoping that one of them would hear my cries and provide a solution to my financial struggles.

Day after day, I continued my prayers, visiting temples in nearby villages and participating in rituals that I hoped would bring about divine intervention. But no matter how much I prayed, nothing changed. My parents remained unable to support my education, and I felt increasingly desperate. It was a time of deep spiritual crisis for me. I began to question whether the gods I had worshiped all my life were truly listening. In my search for a way out of poverty, my mother offered a solution that, at the time, seemed like the only viable option.

3.5.4 A New Direction Suggested

As my family's financial struggles persisted, my mother suggested a path that she believed would offer both stability and spiritual fulfillment. She encouraged me to consider becoming a Hindu temple priest, a role that, in our culture, was both respected and lucrative. My cousin, Symasundera Rao, was a prominent temple priest in the town of Korutla, located in the Karimnagar region of Telangana. He had achieved great wealth and success in his role, and my mother believed that I could follow in his footsteps.

At the time, the idea seemed appealing. Becoming a temple priest would allow me to escape the poverty that had defined my life for so long. It would also provide a sense of spiritual purpose, something that had been important to me since childhood. I imagined myself serving the gods and, in return, being rewarded with financial security.

I decided to approach Symasundera Rao, hoping that he would take me under his wing and guide me toward this new career. I believed that if I could achieve even a fraction of his success, I would be able to provide for my family and live a comfortable life. It seemed like the best option available to me at the time, but little did I know that God had other plans for me.

In the end, while the path of becoming a temple

priest seemed like the ideal solution to both my financial and spiritual longings, life had different plans. What I initially saw as the best way forward was soon revealed to be a temporary option, as God had set me on a course far beyond what I could have imagined. Although I pursued this opportunity with hope, it became clear that the divine purpose for my life extended beyond the security and success I sought at that moment. This realization would ultimately lead me toward a deeper, more profound spiritual calling.

3.5.5 Meeting Nageswarao: A Turning Point

One day, while I was feeling particularly despondent about my future, I happened to stop by a local tailor's shop in my nearby village. The tailor, Kutumbarao, was a kind man, and I had often visited his shop to pass the time. On this particular day, he had a guest—a man named Nageswarao, who was his brother-in-law.

As I sat quietly in the shop, Nageswarao must have noticed the sadness on my face. He asked me why I seemed so troubled, and something about his demeanor made me feel comfortable enough to open up to him. I told him everything—about my dreams of attending college, my family's financial struggles, and the hopelessness I felt as my aspirations seemed to slip away.

To my surprise, Nageswarao didn't dismiss my concerns. Instead, he listened carefully and then offered me a lifeline. He told me about a Christian minority college in Tenali called Ambedkar Junior College. According to him, this college offered opportunities for students like me to get an education without the need for significant financial resources. He said he would be willing to help me gain admission despite my family's financial situation.

It was as if a door had opened in the middle of a dark and seemingly endless hallway. For the first time in months, I felt a sense of hope. Nageswara Rao's offer was unexpected, but it felt like the answer to my prayers—a way for me to pursue my education without being burdened by the limitations of my family's financial situation.

4. A New Beginning: Ambedkar Junior College

True to his word, Nageswarao took immediate action to help me secure a place at Ambedkar Junior College in Tenali. He visited the necessary offices, spoke with the college authorities, and made arrangements for my admission. In a matter of weeks, I found myself standing at the gates of the college, ready to begin a new chapter in my life.

Ambedkar Junior College was a Christian minority institution, and for someone like me, who had grown up in a strictly Hindu environment, it was a completely new world. The college's values of discipline, hard work, and service to others resonated with me deeply. The environment was different from anything I had experienced before, and I soon realized that my entry into this college would not only shape my academic future but also transform my spiritual life.

The college provided me with the opportunity I had been searching for—a chance to pursue my education and build a better future for myself and my family. As I walked through the gates of Ambedkar Junior College, I couldn't help but feel that the gates of heaven had opened for me as well. What had once seemed impossible was now within my reach, and I was determined to make the most of this opportunity. It was the beginning of a new and transformative journey, one that would change the course of my life in ways I could never have imagined.

Joining Ambedkar Junior College for my Intermediate College Education was a defining moment in my life. Specializing in Mathematics, Physics, and Chemistry, I felt my dream of becoming an engineer come closer to reality. Engineering has always fascinated me, and getting accepted into Ambedkar Junior College fulfilled my heart's deepest desire. The rigorous curriculum of science subjects like physics, chemistry, and math provided a solid foundation for my future. I was determined to excel, knowing that a career in engineering could transform my life and provide financial stability for my family. Every day at the college was filled with excitement as I immersed myself in the subjects that I loved, learning from passionate teachers who made complex concepts accessible.

Growing up in a pious Hindu family, I had always been deeply rooted in religious traditions and rituals. Religion was a way of life, and I practiced these rituals with devotion. However, my worldview was limited, and I had never been exposed to any other religious teachings or ideas. My family's beliefs were a significant part of my identity, and I never questioned them.

When I entered Ambedkar Junior College, I found myself in a new environment. Many of the students in the college were Christians, and this introduced me to ideas and perspectives that I had never encountered before. For the first time, I had the opportunity to listen to the teachings of the Bible through my classmates. These interactions sparked a curiosity within me. I was drawn to the message of love, grace, and forgiveness that my Christian peers talked about. Although I was not ready to embrace Christianity, I began to appreciate the values and truths shared in the Bible.

These new spiritual experiences were eye-opening. They were not only lessons in faith but also lessons in humanity. My classmates' kindness, compassion, and humility reflected a different kind of devotion than what I had known. Christianity wasn't just a religion for them; it was a way of life that emphasized love, kindness, and service to others. This exposure to the Christian faith planted seeds of reflection in me that would later play an important role in shaping my spiritual journey. However, at this stage, my focus remained primarily on my studies and my goal to become an engineer.

My journey toward higher education would not have been possible without the constant support of my family, especially my parents. Despite the financial hardships we faced, they always did their best to provide for my education. My father, who had returned from his ascetic life, took on manual labor to ensure that I could pursue my dreams. His sacrifices were a reminder of the responsibilities I carried to succeed and make life better for all of us.

Another key figure in my educational journey was my elder brother, Srinivasa Rao. By the time I had joined Ambedkar Junior College, Srinivasa Rao had secured a position as a professional tailor in Guntur and had started earning a decent income. His financial support was a lifeline for me. Not only did he help cover my educational expenses, but he also provided moral support, encouraging me every step of the way.

Srinivasa Rao's dedication to my education strengthened our bond, and I will always remain grateful for his role in helping me continue my studies. His success was also a source of inspiration for me, pushing me to work harder and achieve my own goals.

At that time, I had one singular goal: to become an engineer and establish myself in a stable and fulfilling career. My focus was unshakable, and I devoted myself entirely to my studies. While other students might have been distracted by social activities or personal pursuits, I had no room for distractions. I knew that the only way to rise above the struggles of my past was to succeed academically. I studied diligently, often late into the night, driven by the hope that education was my key to a better future. The science subjects in my curriculum were challenging, but I found them invigorating. Solving complex equations, understanding the laws of physics, and exploring the chemical interactions that govern the world gave me a sense of purpose and direction. In the two years that I spent at Ambedkar Junior College (1989-1991), my hard work paid off. I performed well in my intermediate exams and earned excellent grades.

A crucial figure in making my dream of education a reality was **Dr. Mannava Rajakishore**, the correspondent of Ambedkar Junior College. Dr. Rajakishore was a man with a vision to empower the marginalized and uplift the oppressed through

Dr. Mannava Rajakishore

education. His commitment to providing affordable education to students from poor and underprivileged backgrounds like me was a blessing. He understood the power of education to transform lives and communities, and his goal was to ensure that even the poorest students had access to quality education.

Dr. Rajakishore's kindness and generosity were evident in the way he structured the fee system at Ambedkar Junior College. The fees were kept incredibly low, which allowed students like me, who came from families with limited means, to continue our studies without worrying about financial burdens. Dr.

Rajakishore's commitment to education as a means of liberation inspired me deeply. His work was a reminder that, while individual effort and perseverance are essential, sometimes all it takes is for someone to extend a helping hand for one's potential to flourish.

Looking back, I realize that the opportunities I received at Ambedkar Junior College were nothing short of miraculous. The support from my family, the exposure to new spiritual ideas, and the affordable education made possible by Dr. Rajakishore all contributed to shaping me into the person I am today. I was surrounded by people who believed in me and wanted to see me succeed. Each of these individuals played a role in guiding me toward the fulfillment of my aspirations.

Without Dr. Rajakishore's vision and compassion, it isn't easy to imagine how I could have continued my education. His efforts remind me that there are people in the world who work tirelessly to uplift others, expecting nothing in return. His dedication to providing education to the marginalized not only transformed my life but also the lives of countless other students like me.

In fact, my time at Ambedkar Junior College was a defining period in my life. It was a time of personal growth, academic achievement, and spiritual exploration. The education I received there laid the foundation for my future and helped me realize that, with determination, support, and faith, anything is possible. My gratitude to Dr. Rajakishore, my family, and my Christian classmates is immeasurable. Their contributions helped open doors that I once thought were beyond my reach.

4.1 A Journey Through Setbacks and Divine Turns

After completing my junior college with Mathematics, Physics, and Chemistry as my primary subjects, I dreamt of pursuing higher education in science. I envisioned myself walking the corridors of universities, studying complex subjects that would pave the way for a rewarding career. My performance in junior college was good, and I believed that my academic success would be the stepping stone toward achieving these dreams. But sometimes, life takes turns we do not anticipate.

As much as I wanted to continue my education, financial constraints loomed large over my dreams. My family, particularly my mother, had already endured so much, and now, with the weight of supporting my education, the pressure became unbearable. My father's unemployment had left us without any stable means of financial support, and the little income my family had was spent on basic needs. The idea of further studies seemed like a luxury we could no longer afford.

With a heavy heart, I had to let go of my aspirations for higher education and return to my village, Salempalem. The day I left the city and returned to the familiar, dusty streets of my village felt like a defeat. The dreams I once held so close felt like they were slipping out of reach. The future seemed uncertain, and for the first time in my life, I felt utterly directionless.

4.2 Learning a New Skill

Back in Salempalem, reality hit me hard. I couldn't just sit idle and mourn my lost opportunities. I needed to find a way to contribute to my family and make a living. With no immediate prospects for education, I turned to a skill that could offer me some means of survival—tailoring. There was a nearby village where I heard about a tailoring workshop, and though it wasn't the path I had envisioned, it was something I could learn and perhaps use to earn a living.

For six long months, I walked barefoot to this neighboring village every day. The journey was both physically and emotionally taxing. The rough, uneven paths would often cut into my feet, and with every step, I was reminded of the dreams I had left behind. But I pressed on, determined to make the most of what was before me. I learned the craft of stitching pants and shirts, slowly acquiring the skills necessary to become a competent tailor.

The mornings would begin with the sound of roosters crowing in the distance, and I would set off, the sun just beginning to rise over the fields. As I walked, I thought about the friends I had left behind in the city—those who were still pursuing their studies while I was learning to measure fabric and handle a sewing machine. It wasn't the life I wanted, but it was the life I had.

Tailoring didn't come naturally to me at first. The delicate balance between precision and creativity that was required took time to master. But I persisted. Every day, I focused on learning the details—how to cut fabric perfectly, how to stitch clean seams, and how to ensure that the clothes fit just right. My hands became calloused from handling the materials, but my skills improved.

A New Opportunity in Guntur

After six months of training in the village, I decided it was time to put my new skills to use. My brother, Srinivasa Rao, was living in Guntur at the time, and he suggested that I move there to find work in a proper tailoring shop. With no better options, I packed my belongings and made the move to Guntur, hopeful that this city might offer me some new possibilities.

Through my brother's help, I found a job at a tailoring shop called SM Tailors in Kothapet, Guntur. The shop owner, Meera, quickly became not just my boss but also a mentor. He was kind and patient, taking the time to help me improve my craft. Under his guidance, I honed my skills further, and for a while, tailoring became my life. Meera was more than just an employer; he was a teacher. He saw potential in me, and through his guidance, I began to see it in myself too.

But no matter how much I learned or how skilled I became, there was a persistent ache in my heart. Every time I saw my old friends—those who had been my classmates during junior college—walking through the streets of Guntur with their heads buried in books, I felt a pang of envy and sorrow. Many of them were now pursuing higher education in colleges, exactly where I had hoped to be. The stark contrast between their lives and mine was painful.

I often found myself crying out to an unknown God. The desire to continue my education never left me, despite the path I had taken. My hands were busy stitching clothes, but my heart longed for the life I had once imagined. Every stitch I made seemed to be sewing up a wound in my soul, but the desire for knowledge and growth still burned inside me.

A Divine Encounter

One year passed this way—working, learning, and living in Guntur. But as the days wore on, discontent grew in me. I found myself agonizing over my situation, feeling trapped and unable to see a way forward. Just when I thought my dream of returning to education was fading, an unexpected encounter changed everything.

One day, while walking through the streets of Guntur, I ran into Mr. Nageswara Rao. He was the same man who had previously helped me with my junior college education. The surprise on his face when he saw me working in a tailoring shop was palpable. He immediately asked me why I wasn't attending college, and I explained my situation—the financial struggles, the lack of support, and my inability to continue my studies.

To my amazement, Mr. Nageswara Rao brought me good news. He told me that Ambedkar College in Tenali, the same college where I had studied intermediate, had opened new programs offering higher degrees. Not only that, but he was willing to help me get admission and support me financially.

The moment felt surreal. After so many months of hopelessness, the possibility of returning to college seemed like a distant dream. But here it was, an opportunity handed to me once again. Though my heart had always been inclined toward the sciences, the only option available at Ambedkar College was a Bachelor of Arts in English Literature. I hesitated at first, feeling a disconnect from my passion for science, but I knew I had to seize the opportunity that God had placed before me.

A New Path in English Literature

Reluctantly, I accepted admission into the BA in English Literature program. Though it wasn't the field I had dreamed of studying, it was a step forward, and for that, I was grateful. Once again, I found myself immersed in the world of academia, but this time, it felt different. The sciences, with their precision and logic, had always captured my interest, but now I was stepping into the world of language, literature, and philosophy—subjects I hadn't considered before.

During this time, I was fortunate to meet again Dr. Rajkishore, the college's correspondent. Like a father figure, he welcomed me into the college and even arranged for me to stay in the hostel. His kindness and support were yet another reminder that God was watching over me, guiding my steps even when I couldn't see the full picture. I was grateful to him for offering me a place not just to study, but to live—a stable environment where I could focus on my education without the constant worry of financial strain.

4.3 Spiritual Awakening and Revelation

As I delved deeper into my studies, something profound began to happen within me. The discontent and agony that had weighed me down for so long started to dissipate. It was during this period that my spiritual journey took a new direction. My life, once dominated by worldly concerns and ambitions, began to turn toward the eternal. I realized that God had been with me all along, guiding me through each challenge and hardship.

This realization marked a significant turning point in my life. The desire to succeed in the eyes of the world gave way to a deeper yearning—to know God more intimately and to seek His will in everything I did. My journey of faith had begun, and it was a journey that would shape the rest of my life.

What began as a struggle for survival and education had now transformed into something far greater—a spiritual awakening that would lead me to discover my true purpose. This new chapter of my life, filled with faith and trust in God, is a story that will continue in the next part of this autobiography.

During my time at Dr. B. R. Ambedkar Degree College in Tenali, Andhra Pradesh, my academic life seemed to be going smoothly on the surface, yet restlessness gnawed at me from within. While I pursued my BA in English literature, a thirst for a deeper understanding of life—of the ultimate truth— grew stronger every day. It was as if a quiet, unexpressed longing burned within me, seeking something far beyond the intellectual exercises of my studies. I had a silent dialogue with the unknown Almighty God, a yearning that no amount of books or discussions could satisfy. The search for truth had already become the primary theme of my inner life, although I wasn't sure where this path would lead.

I came from a tradition deeply rooted in ancient wisdom and rituals, and like many of my peers, I was proud of my Hindu heritage. My connection to the Hindu Scriptures and to the practices of my ancestors was strong, and I carried within me a sense of cultural superiority. This was a natural extension of my caste consciousness, an inheritance passed down through generations. As an orthodox Hindu, I viewed the world from a specific lens—one that often placed our practices and traditions on a pedestal.

Despite being surrounded by students who practiced other faiths, especially Christianity, I maintained a distance from their beliefs. Christian friends from my college would occasionally ask me to read their holy book, the Bible, but I rejected it outright. I found it difficult to respect a faith whose followers, from my observation, did not always live up to the ideals they professed. In fact, I saw many Christian students engaging in behavior that I judged harshly—fighting, smoking, wasting their time with movies, and some even indulging in behaviors that bordered on the immoral. This only strengthened my disdain for their faith, as I believed I was morally superior. I couldn't see how their religious text could possibly offer anything of value when their lifestyle seemed so far from righteous.

There was also an intellectual and cultural pride born from my caste that contributed to this rejection. Like many others of my background, I assumed that Christianity was a lesser faith, foreign and unrelated to the lofty teachings of our dharma. The very idea that I, an orthodox Hindu who had been raised with the Vedic wisdom, should consider the teachings of another tradition seemed absurd. I was conscious of the societal hierarchy that placed me and my people in positions of spiritual and intellectual authority, and this pride did not allow me to even consider the possibility of reading the Bible.

It was a curious paradox for me. I was, by nature, a voracious reader. I have been a voracious reader of books since I was a little child, enjoying everything from contemporary fiction and literature to the classics of Hindu philosophy. I had a hunger for knowledge, and the sight of any book sparked my interest. Yet, the Bible—though it had been offered to me numerous times—remained untouched. It wasn't a deliberate avoidance at first, but over time it became a conscious decision. I would not waste my time reading a book from a tradition I had already deemed inferior.

But then something changed, and I cannot fully explain why. It was August 1993, and it seemed like any other Friday. The college hostel was quiet, with most students out enjoying the holiday. I was alone in my room with nothing particular to do, and I felt the familiar restlessness creep in. On my friend's table, as it had been for weeks, lay a small blue book—Gideon's New Testament. I had seen it countless times before, but that day something was different. I was drawn to it, despite myself.

There was an inner struggle. Part of me, the proud voice of my upbringing, told me to ignore it, to walk away. What could this book possibly offer me? But another part of me, a deeper instinct perhaps, urged me to open it. This was not the first time I had felt such a conflict, but it was stronger than before. After a few moments of hesitation, I reached out and picked up the book. My heart pounded as I held it in my hands, and I felt as though I had crossed an invisible boundary— one that I had never even realized existed.

I opened the book to the first page of the Gospel of Matthew, and what I read surprised me. It began with a genealogy—a list of names tracing the lineage of a man called Jesus, all the way back through generations. This immediately struck a chord within me. As a member of a tradition that holds ancestry in high regard, the concept of a divine being with a traceable genealogy was captivating. In Hinduism, we are often deeply conscious of our ancestors, our lineages, and the roles they play in shaping who we are. The idea that God himself could have a lineage fascinated me. I had never before considered that the divine might choose to incarnate in a form so deeply connected to human history.

As I continued to read, time seemed to stand still. The words on the page, though foreign, carried a weight that I had not anticipated. The story of God taking on human form began to make sense to me in a way I had not expected. Hindu philosophy is filled with the concept of avatars—divine beings who descend to earth to restore dharma. The more I read, the more I began to see parallels between what was in the Bible and what I had known all my life. Yet, this was different. There was a simplicity in this narrative, a humility to the idea that God would not only take on a human form but would live and walk among ordinary people.

As I read through the Gospel of Matthew, one verse in particular stopped me in my tracks. It was Matthew 5:20: "For I tell you that unless your righteousness surpasses that of the Pharisees and the teachers of the law, you will certainly not enter the kingdom of heaven." In the Telugu translation, the term for the "teachers of the law" was "*Sastri* (శాస్త్రి)"—a

term that hit close to home for me. In the caste hierarchy, I was a Sastri, part of the priestly class, the custodians of religious knowledge. This verse shook me to the core. It seemed to suggest that simply being a keeper of tradition, simply following the law, was not enough. There was a higher standard, a greater truth that went beyond the rituals and rules I had been taught to hold sacred.

That night, I could not sleep. The words I had read continued to echo in my mind. My identity, my caste, my culture—everything I had believed about who I was and what was important—was being challenged by a text I had dismissed for so long. The Bible, which I had thought contained nothing of value for me, now seemed to be speaking directly to my deepest questions, my unexpressed fears, and my restless search for truth.

As I lay in bed, I felt a mix of fear and

excitement. I knew, in a way I couldn't yet articulate, that what I had read was significant. It wasn't just a religious text. It was a mirror, reflecting back at me not only the truths I had avoided but also the path I had been seeking all along. The pride I had carried for so long was beginning to crack, and in its place, a new understanding was emerging—a realization that truth was not confined to the boundaries I had constructed around myself.

I did not know what the future held, but one thing was clear: my encounter with the Bible that day had opened a door within me. It challenged my assumptions and forced me to confront the possibility that the truth I sought might not be confined to the traditions I had grown up with. My search was far from over, but for the first time in my life, I felt as though I was on the right path, guided not by pride or arrogance, but by a genuine desire to know the truth, no matter where it came from.

It was a restless Friday night. Questions swirled in my mind, like a storm stirring up the calm sea of my thoughts. The struggle from the day before, the encounter with the Bible, had left me unsettled. Sleep was elusive, and when it finally came, it was not the restful sleep I had hoped for. My body rested, but my mind was still racing.

Early the next morning, at around 5 a.m., I was abruptly pulled from sleep by my classmate, Rathaiah. He yanked the blanket off me, shaking me from my slumber, and with an eager voice, he urged me to join him for a university students' camp—a simple outing, he said. His timing could not have been worse, and though I was upset at being woken up so early, the idea of getting away from my thoughts and routine seemed like a good distraction. I agreed, thinking it was a normal student trip to relax, spend time outdoors, and perhaps enjoy some peace away from the usual academic grind.

As we traveled, the fresh air of the early morning began to clear my mind. We soon arrived at a small village called Nambur, not far from Acharya Nagarjuna University in Guntur. As we stepped off the bus, I began noticing something peculiar. Several students around us were carrying small books in their hands—Bibles. It hit me like a jolt. This wasn't a simple outing. Rathaiah had brought me to a Christian student camp, and I immediately suspected that his intention was to convert me. A deep sense of betrayal and frustration welled up inside me.

The thought of staying there felt unbearable. I didn't want to be drawn into a place where I would be pressured to adopt a belief system I had resisted for so long. My instinct was to run, to leave the camp as quickly as I could. But as I looked around, I realized that I was stuck. The village was small and remote, and by the time we arrived, the evening was already closing in. It was dark, and there was no way I could make my way back to the hostel alone. With a sense of resignation, I decided to stay, though my heart was heavy with reluctance.

That evening, I found myself walking with the other students toward a meeting hall where the camp's activities were to take place. My feet moved, but my spirit resisted. I was filled with negative thoughts— suspicion, even a little fear. As I approached the building, I expected to find some grand, holy structure, like the ornate temples I was accustomed to, where every corner would reflect the sacred. But the place I found was different, entirely ordinary. It was a plain, unfinished building with nothing special about it, nothing that suggested it was a place of profound spiritual importance. There were no statues, no incense, no elaborate rituals.

As we climbed to the top floor, which was nothing more than a roof with four pillars and no walls, I began to feel a little more at ease. The cool breeze gently touched my face, and the simplicity of the surroundings calmed my mind. The openness of the space, with its unfinished corners, felt natural and unpretentious. There was no grandiosity here, nothing imposing, and in that simplicity, I began to relax.

When we entered the hall, something unusual caught my attention. **Sri. Suresh Vinod Kumar**, the singing (*Bhajan*) teacher for the evening was seated in a lotus position (*padmasana*), just like a sage in meditation. His posture immediately reminded me of our own teachers and spiritual guides, those who sat with quiet dignity to impart wisdom. He had a large *sitar* in his hands, a musical instrument I loved deeply for its connection to our classical traditions. The scene felt oddly familiar, almost like home, and all of the foreignness I had associated with that religion began to dissolve. For the first time in a long while, I didn't feel out of place. My apprehensions faded, and I sat down willingly, curious about what this man would teach.

The session began, and to my surprise, the words spoken were not as alien to me as I had imagined. They spoke of divine truths—of life, of existence, of the nature of humanity—that resonated with the questions that had been haunting me. As I listened, it wasn't the external doctrines or religious jargon that struck me. It was something deeper, a connection to the same truths I had been seeking in my own way for so long.

The teachings that evening centered around the nature of life, the essence of the divine, and the condition of the human soul. The speaker's words echoed truths that were familiar to me, but they were presented in a way that made me see them in a new light. The conversation turned toward the concept of sin—something I had always understood differently. In my tradition, the idea of karma, of actions having consequences, was central. But here, they spoke of the inner condition of the soul, of how we fall short not just in actions but in our very nature. This idea intrigued me, though I resisted it at first.

As the evening went on, the teacher invited the students to reflect on what had been shared, and then something unexpected happened. He made what he called an "altar call," inviting those who wanted to commit to a higher spiritual path to raise their hands. Many of the students around me responded immediately, lifting their hands in agreement. But I sat still, my mind racing. I was moved by what I had heard, but fear held me back. Fear of what my family would think, fear of what my community would say, fear of the cultural weight I carried. My upbringing, my caste, my heritage—they all stood like guards around my heart, telling me that this was not my path.

But something inside me had already begun to change. It wasn't something any human being could convince me of, not something forced upon me by external persuasion. There was a quiet voice, deep within, that spoke to me with an authority I couldn't ignore. I realized that what I had been searching for all along, the truth that had eluded me in books, rituals, and intellectual pursuits, had come to me in this unexpected way. It wasn't about abandoning my heritage or rejecting my culture—it was about finding the ultimate reality that transcended all of it.

That night, on the 7th of August 1993, I reached a point of no return. I knew, deep in my soul, that I had encountered something that would change my life forever. It was not a decision made out of emotion or excitement but a quiet, unshakable conviction that I had found the truth. It was as though a veil had been lifted, and everything became clear. The divine had revealed Himself to me, not in a foreign way, but in a way that spoke directly to my heart, answering the deepest questions I had carried for so long.

After the meeting ended, I felt an overwhelming need to be alone. I skipped dinner and found a solitary spot among some bushes, away from the crowd. Without even thinking, I knelt down, my heart overflowing with a sense of reverence and awe. Words of prayer, though unfamiliar in this new context, poured out from me, directed toward the divine presence I had encountered.

At that moment, I experienced something beyond description. It was as if the entire weight of my past—the pride, the fears, the confusion—was lifted from me. What remained was a profound sense of peace, a rest that I had never known before. It was as if the very essence of heaven had entered my weary soul, bringing with it a clarity and serenity I had longed for but never found. The ultimate reality, which I had sought in so many ways, had come to me not in a temple, not through a ritual, but in the quietness of my heart, in the person of the divine itself.

When I returned to the hostel in Tenali after the camp, I knew that there was no turning back. The journey I had begun that weekend was one that would shape the rest of my life. The search for truth had led me to an unexpected place, but it was the place I had been seeking all along.

4.4 A Newfound Spiritual Path

When I returned to my hostel room in Tenali after the spiritual retreat at Nambur camp, I carried a deep sense of inner peace and joy that was completely new to me. I had been searching for something greater, and during the camp, I found it in the form of an awakening. This inner peace, this newfound connection to the divine, filled me with a happiness I had never known before. It felt as though the truth I had been seeking for so long had finally found me. But even amidst this peace, I couldn't shake the subtle fear that clung to my mind.

Growing up in an orthodox Hindu family, the values, traditions, and beliefs were deeply ingrained in me. My family and community had always followed these ways, and I couldn't help but wonder how they would respond to the transformation I had experienced. Would they accept me? Or would they reject this newfound path that I had embraced? These questions haunted me, even as I tried to focus on the peace I had discovered.

A Quest for Inner Confirmation

Although my experience at the camp had been real, and I knew deep in my heart that I had encountered the divine in a way I had never imagined, my soul still craved confirmation. My mind, still influenced by the teachings and beliefs of my upbringing, questioned the authenticity of my experience. Was it truly the divine calling me? Or was it just my imagination? These doubts were not unfamiliar to me, but this time, they felt heavier.

I needed something more—some assurance, some confirmation that what I had felt was real and that it was leading me toward the path of truth. I wanted a direct encounter with the divine, something that would leave no room for doubt. The longing in my soul grew stronger with each passing day, and I found myself turning more and more to prayer, seeking answers.

An Early Morning of Struggle and Revelation

It was in the quiet stillness of an October morning in 1993 that my longing for divine assurance reached its peak. It was 4 a.m., and as had been my custom since childhood, I rose early for my morning prayers. Growing up, I had always observed this time of day as sacred, a time for offering puja, chanting mantras, and seeking the blessings of the gods. But on this particular morning, there was a different energy within me. I was eager, excited, and yet anxious. My mind was restless with thoughts of my upcoming visit to my village of Salempalem, where I would have to face my family with this new spiritual awareness I had embraced.

As I sat in prayer, my heart was heavy with questions. I was young, barely out of my teenage years, and I felt unprepared to confront the expectations of my family and community. How would they react to this new path I had chosen? Would they understand? Would they see the beauty and truth I had found? Or would they see it as a betrayal of our family's deeply held traditions? These thoughts weighed heavily on me, and I struggled to find peace as I prayed.

The Divine Voice That Called My Name

It was during this inner turmoil that something extraordinary happened. As I sat in the quiet of the early morning, pouring out my fears and doubts in prayer, I heard a voice. It was not a voice I had ever heard before, and yet it was familiar in a way that words cannot describe. It called out a name: **Jeremiah**. I heard it clearly in my native Telugu language, . The voice came to me not once, but three times, each time growing louder and more insistent.

The word **Jeremiah** echoed in my mind, but I was perplexed. What was this name? I had never heard it before, neither in my Hindu upbringing nor in the spiritual experiences I had encountered so far. The name felt foreign, yet there was an undeniable power behind it. I wondered if it was a trick of my mind, an illusion brought on by my overactive imagination. But the more I thought about it, the more the word **Jeremiah** reverberated in my consciousness, like the ringing of a temple bell.

Doubt and Mental Conflict

I spent the rest of the day in a state of confusion. I went to my college classes, but I could not focus on the lectures. The word **Jeremiah** kept echoing in my mind, and I began to question my own sanity. Was I imagining things? Was there something wrong with me? The more I tried to push the thought aside, the more persistent it became. It was as if the name was etched into my soul, and no matter how hard I tried, I could not escape it.

I began to worry that perhaps I was experiencing a psychological breakdown. Hearing voices and strange words that I had never encountered before—it all seemed too strange, too unsettling. I felt lost and uncertain about what was happening to me. Was it a sign from the divine, or was my mind playing tricks on me? I couldn't be sure.

A Friend's Surprising Response

By the end of the day, I couldn't keep this inner

conflict to myself any longer. I decided to confide in a spiritual friend, someone I trusted. I wasn't sure how to explain the situation, but I knew I needed answers. When I told him about the name **Jeremiah**, he smiled, as though he knew exactly what I was talking about. His calm response surprised me. He didn't seem confused or worried. Instead, he simply suggested that I read the Old Testament, where I would find the name **Jeremiah**.

I was both relieved and curious. Could this be the answer I had been seeking? Could this mysterious word that had been haunting me have a deeper meaning? My friend's suggestion ignited a new sense of urgency within me, and I hurried back to my hostel, eager to uncover the truth.

The Search for the Meaning of Jeremiah

Back at my hostel, I encountered a new challenge. I only had a copy of the New Testament, specifically the Gospel of John, which had been given to me during my initial exploration of this new faith. I had been told by those guiding me that I should focus on John's gospel for at least a year before venturing into the rest of the scriptures. Reading the Old

Testament, they said, was something that could wait until I had a stronger foundation in my new faith.

But in that moment, my need for answers was stronger than any restrictions. I found another friend who had a full Bible and asked him for a copy. I eagerly opened the table of contents and searched for the name **Jeremiah**. When I found it, I quickly turned to the first chapter, my heart racing with anticipation. What I discovered in the pages of the Old Testament would change my life forever.

The Divine Message in Jeremiah 1:5-10

As I began reading Jeremiah 1:5-10, I felt an immediate connection to the words on the page. It was as if the divine was speaking directly to me through the ancient text. "Before I formed you in the womb, I knew you," the verse began. "Before you were born, I set you apart; I appointed you as a prophet to the nations." These words resonated deeply within me. They answered the very questions I had been struggling with. Like the prophet Jeremiah, I had been questioning my worth, my purpose, and whether I was too young and inexperienced to embrace this new spiritual path. But here, in this sacred text, the divine was assuring me that

I had been chosen for a purpose long before I was even born. I had been set apart, and the path I was on was no accident—it was part of a divine plan.

Overcoming Self-Doubt with Divine Assurance

The words in Jeremiah 1:5-10 continued to speak to my heart. Jeremiah himself had doubted his ability to fulfill the calling placed on his life. "I do not know how to speak; I am too young," he had said. These were my own thoughts, my own fears. I had been wrestling with the same doubts, feeling inadequate and unprepared for the journey ahead. But just as the divine had reassured Jeremiah, I too found comfort in the words: "Do not say, 'I am too young.' You must go to everyone I send you to and say whatever I command you."

In that moment, I realized that my fears of facing my family and society, with my newfound spiritual awareness, were unfounded. The divine had spoken directly to my soul, reassuring me that my youth and inexperience were not obstacles, but rather part of a greater purpose. I was being called to walk this path, regardless of my age or background, and I was not walking it alone. The presence of the Almighty was with me, guiding me every step of the way.

4.5 Finding Strength in Divine Promises

The final verses of Jeremiah 1:5-10 were a powerful affirmation of what I had longed for assurance and protection. "Do not be afraid of them, for I am with you and will rescue you," the divine voice said. These words struck me with such clarity and power that all my lingering doubts began to dissolve. The Almighty was promising not only to guide me but to protect me from any challenges I might face, whether from my family, society, or my own inner fears.

This moment was transformative. I no longer questioned the validity of my spiritual experience or the direction my life was taking. The divine had spoken directly to me, through sacred text, and I knew that I was walking the path that had been set for me long before I even understood its significance. My soul was at peace, and the fear that had plagued me for weeks was finally lifted.

4.6 A Divine Encounter That Changed Everything

As I closed the Bible that evening, I felt a deep sense of gratitude and awe. What I had experienced was more than just a personal revelation—it was a divine encounter that had confirmed everything I had been seeking. The voice I had heard in the early hours of the morning, the name **Jeremiah** that had echoed in my mind, was no illusion or trick of the mind. It was the Almighty reaching out to me, guiding me, and preparing me for the journey ahead.

This experience marked a turning point in my spiritual life. The doubts that had once clouded my mind were gone, replaced by a sense of purpose and clarity. I no longer feared the reactions of my family or the expectations of society. I knew that the divine had chosen me and that this path, though challenging, was where I was meant to be.

Returning to Salempalem with Confidence

As the days passed and the time to return to my family in Salempalem grew nearer to the *Dasara festival*, I found myself filled with quiet confidence. The fear of how my parents and relatives would react to my newfound faith had been replaced by a deep trust in the divine. I no longer felt the need to justify or explain my spiritual transformation. I knew that the

Almighty was with me, guiding my every step, and that gave me the strength to face whatever lay ahead.

When I finally returned home to spend my holidays, I was greeted with the warmth and familiarity of my childhood. But beneath the surface, there was a sense of distance. My parents and relatives could sense that something had changed in me. They didn't fully understand it, and there were moments of tension and unease as they tried to reconcile the person I had become with the person they had always known.

Facing Family and Tradition

My family's expectations were clear. We came from a long line of devout Hindus, and our traditions were deeply woven into the fabric of our lives. My relatives had always assumed that I would follow the same path, embracing the rituals, customs, and beliefs that had been passed down through generations. But the path I was now walking was different, and I knew that this difference would not go unnoticed.

At first, I hesitated to speak openly about my spiritual transformation. I wanted to respect my family's traditions and avoid causing any unnecessary conflict. But as the days went by, it became clear that I could not hide the truth of what had happened to me. I could not deny the reality of the divine encounter that had changed my life. And so, slowly, I began to share my story.

A Clash of Worlds

The first conversations with my parents about my spiritual awakening were challenging, to say the least. The moment I revealed that I had embraced a new path, I could see confusion and dismay wash over their faces. My father, especially, could not comprehend why I had chosen to follow a different spiritual tradition from the one we had observed for generations. Our family was steeped in a rich heritage of devotion and worship, with deities who had been revered for centuries. The rituals, festivals, and prayers had not just been religious practices; they were woven into the very fabric of our identity as a family.

For my father, it wasn't just a matter of faith; it was about honor, tradition, and the continuity of our lineage. He saw my spiritual shift as a betrayal, not only to him personally but to the gods who had blessed our family. In his eyes, I was abandoning the very source of our well-being. My mother, although less vocal than my father, also struggled to accept this change. She was a woman of devotion, committed to the daily rituals and sacred practices that had defined her life. For her, the gods had always been protective, and this new path of mine felt like a step into uncertainty.

Both my parents were deeply aware of the social and cultural implications of my decision. In our community, turning away from the established religious norms could mean alienation, gossip, and dishonor. My father was a man of respect, known for his strict adherence to the family's religious duties. Now, his son's actions seemed to cast a shadow on that reputation. The weight of communal judgment bore heavily on him, and he made it clear that this was not just a private matter but a public one, one that could affect the standing of our family.

My Father's Anger

As days passed, my father's anger began to intensify. He was a man of discipline, with clear expectations for his family, and I had crossed a line that he never anticipated. The conversations became arguments, and his frustration often manifested in threats of physical violence. Several times, I found myself cornered by his fury. He would raise his hand to strike me, overwhelmed by the need to correct what he saw as my disobedience and disrespect. I could see the pain in his eyes, the anguish of a father who believed his son had lost his way.

But every time he came close to raising his hand, my mother intervened. She, too, was heartbroken by my decision, but her love for me overshadowed her confusion. She could not bear the thought of her son being hurt, no matter how much she disagreed with my choices. Time and again, she would stand between us, gently reminding my father that violence was not the answer. Her presence was my shield during those heated moments, and though she did not understand my path, her love for me remained steadfast.

A Month of Turmoil

I had come home for a month, hoping to rest and reconnect with my family. What I found instead was a household in turmoil. The peace that once filled our home had been replaced by tension and unease. My parents were constantly on edge, and every conversation seemed to spiral into a discussion about my spiritual choices. My siblings, too, were confused and didn't know how to respond. The harmony that once defined our family life was disrupted, replaced by an atmosphere of suspicion and unresolved conflict.

In those days, I found solace in the sacred texts that had now become my guide. As I read, I was reminded of an ancient teaching that spoke of how families would be divided, that fathers would turn against their sons and sons against their fathers. What I was experiencing at home was the fulfillment of this prophecy. I understood then that my spiritual journey was not just about personal transformation but also about navigating the challenges that came with it, even if it meant facing the pain of familial division. This realization gave me the strength to endure the emotional and psychological battles at home.

Seeking Refuge in Solitude

With the opposition at home growing stronger, I found myself needing a place of quiet, where I could connect with the divine in peace. That place became the thorny bushes outside the village. Every day, I would slip away from the house and find refuge among those bushes, far from the eyes of my family and the villagers. It was a secluded spot, rough and unwelcoming to most, but for me, it became a sanctuary where I could immerse myself in the sacred scriptures without interruption.

It was during this time of secret reading that I found profound lessons in the stories 1 and 2 Kings books of the Bible. These kings, revered for their wisdom and power, often began their reigns with noble intentions. However, many of them succumbed to temptation, allowing their early righteousness to be eroded by pride and ambition. This deeply resonated with me. I understood that my spiritual journey was not just about starting well but about finishing well. The stories of these kings became cautionary tales, urging me to remain vigilant, to guard against complacency, and to stay true to my path till the very end.

The Divine Presence

As I spent more time in solitude, reading and reflecting, I began to feel a profound closeness to the divine. The turmoil at home no longer seemed overwhelming because I could sense a higher power guiding me, comforting me, and assuring me of its presence. Day by day, I felt my faith deepening, and I began to enjoy a peace that surpassed my understanding. The opposition I faced at home, rather than breaking me, only served to strengthen my resolve. I knew that the divine hand was upon me, shaping my path.

Those one month at home, though filled with conflict, became a period of significant spiritual growth. I saw the divine hand at work in every situation, and this filled me with an unshakable faith. The tension in my family did not deter me; rather, it solidified my belief that I was walking the right path. I had no doubt that the Almighty was with me, guiding me through these trials and preparing me for the journey ahead.

Financial Trials and Divine Provision

As the holidays came to an end, I prepared to return to my college hostel. But this time, I was going back with nothing. My father, still angry at my decisions, had cut off all financial support. He believed that by applying this kind of pressure, I would be forced to reconsider my spiritual path. It was a test of my commitment, a way to see if I would abandon this new faith under the weight of practical concerns. But I was not afraid. Material needs, I knew, could not deter me from the truth I had found.

With no money in hand, I returned to college, fully trusting that the Almighty would provide for my needs. And this is where the story takes a remarkable turn. What happened next was nothing short of miraculous. I began to see the divine's provision in ways I had never expected. From the kindness of strangers to unexpected opportunities, I found that my needs were met at every turn. It became clear to me that the divine was not only a distant force but an active presence in my life, orchestrating events to ensure my well-being. As I look back now, I see that this chapter of my life was one of divine intervention and provision. Despite the opposition from my family and the financial pressures that came with it, I was never truly alone. The Almighty's hand was guiding me every step of the way, providing for my needs and giving me the strength to persevere. Keep reading to discover how, even in the face of adversity, my journey continued to unfold, and how the divine's provision manifested in ways that continue to inspire me to this day.

Divine Provision Amidst Loneliness

The journey I embarked upon as a young student was neither easy nor without its share of challenges. Yet, I can see now, as I reflect on those early days, how Almighty God gently but surely directed my steps. Like a newborn baby crying out for nourishment, I experienced a deep and insatiable thirst for spiritual growth. My heart opened wide to the Word of God, and I developed a hunger for His presence that only grew stronger with time.

As the holidays ended and I returned to my hostel, I began to experience a profound shift in my spiritual life. The world outside might have seen me as a simple, lonely student, struggling to make ends meet, but within, I was being molded by the Almighty to fight the battle of loneliness. Though I often felt alone in my circumstances, I was not afraid. I had been trained by God from my childhood to face difficulties head-on. I had faced abandonment, poverty, and the weight of rejection, and each challenge had made me stronger and more reliant on God's grace.

When I returned to the hostel after the holidays, I was penniless. I needed pocket money, not just for basic sustenance, but to pay for my books, my hostel fees, and my tuition at Ambedkar College. Though it wasn't as expensive as some of the other institutions, I had no means to pay. It was a difficult and humbling time. Yet, even as I grappled with these harsh realities, I knew that the God who had called me would not abandon me.

A Divine Appointment at Mr. Mark's Home

In those days, there were moments when the weight of my financial burdens felt overwhelming. But it was during one of these moments that I attended a prayer meeting at Mr. Mark's home in Chenchupet, Tenali. Mr. Mark was a loving and kind teacher who welcomed students like me into his home for fellowship and prayer. Little did I know that this seemingly ordinary meeting would turn into a life-changing experience.

After the meeting, Mr. Mark prayed for me, as was his custom. But something unusual happened that day. As we finished praying, he handed me a small cover. Inside, there was Rs. 20—a seemingly modest amount, but for me, it was as if the floodgates of heaven had opened. I hadn't shared my financial struggles with anyone, yet God knew my every need and prompted Mr. Mark to give me exactly what I needed at that moment.

The Rs. 20 allowed me to buy food, which I was desperately in need of, and purchase an essential English literature book for my studies. That day, I realized in a very tangible way that God's provision is perfect, even in the smallest of details. This experience boosted my faith, reinforcing the truth that God, who created the universe out of nothing, was more than capable of providing for me in my time of need.

The Birth of an Idea: Finding a Part-Time Job

With my immediate needs met, I began to think more practically about how I could sustain myself moving forward. While I was grateful for Mr. Mark's gift, I knew that I couldn't rely solely on the generosity of others. I needed a steady source of income to cover my hostel and college fees.

One day, while praying for guidance, a thought came to me: I could use a skill I had learned earlier— tailoring. Now, the skill I learned during my study break, that skill came back to mind as a possible way to support myself.

At that time, our college classes at Ambedkar College ran from 7:30 AM to 12:20 PM, leaving the rest of the day free. I realized that if I could find part-time work as a tailor in the afternoons, I might be able to earn enough to cover my basic needs. I didn't have much experience in navigating the professional world, but I knew that God had given me this idea, and I trusted that He would open doors for me.

A Relentless Search for Employment

Armed with this newfound determination, I set out one afternoon, walking along Bose Road in Tenali, where many tailoring shops were located. I visited shop after shop, explaining my situation and asking if they had any part-time work available.

Most of the shop owners were skeptical. When they learned I was a degree student at Ambedkar College, they doubted my sincerity. In that part of India, it was uncommon for college students to work, particularly in skilled trades like tailoring. Most of the tailors were uneducated and, often, they had fallen into bad habits.

Shop owners would ask me about my background—who my parents were, where I lived, and why I needed a job. When I explained that my father had stopped supporting me due to a conflict over my newfound Biblical faith, many of them became angry. They would tell me to return home and be obedient to my parents. They didn't understand my spiritual journey or the deep conviction I had to follow the path Almighty God had set before me.

Despite the rejection, I didn't give up. For nearly two weeks, I walked from shop to shop, searching for someone who would give me a chance. Each day, I prayed for God's guidance and trusted that He had a plan, even though I couldn't see it yet.

An Open Door at Yax Ciny Tailoring Shop

On the 11th day, I walked into a shop called "Yax Ciny Tailoring," also located on Bose Road. The owner, Srinivasa Rao, was different from the other shop owners I had encountered. He listened to my story patiently, without interrupting or passing judgment. When I finished explaining my situation—how I was a student in need of work, how my father had stopped supporting me because of my faith—he surprised me by offering me a part-time job.

I can still remember the joy I felt at that

moment. After so many days of rejection, God had finally opened a door for me. Srinivasa Rao was willing to take a chance on me, even though I was a student, and even though my circumstances were unconventional.

From that day forward, my life took on a new rhythm. I would attend college in the morning, then head to Yax Ciny Tailoring in the afternoon to work. I stitched clothes, learning more and more with each passing day. It wasn't always easy, but I knew that God had provided this opportunity for me, and I was determined to make the most of it.

A New Chapter in Faith and Provision

Looking back, I can see how God used those difficult days to shape me into the person I am today. Each rejection, each moment of loneliness, was part of His divine plan to prepare me for greater things. He provided for me in ways I could never have imagined, from the unexpected gift from Mr. Mark to the job offer from Srinivasa Rao. Through it all, my faith was strengthened, and I learned to trust in God's provision, no matter the circumstances.

The adventure of working at Yax Ciny

Tailoring was just the beginning of a new chapter in my journey. As I continued to walk in faith, I discovered that the more I trusted in God, the more He revealed His power and grace in my life. Every challenge became an opportunity to experience His goodness, and every step forward was a testament to His unfailing love.

This part of my life, though filled with struggles, was also filled with hope. It was during these days that I truly began to understand what it meant to live by faith, to rely on the Almighty for every need, and to see His hand at work in the most unexpected ways.

5. Faith Awakens in Tenali: My EU Journey
A New Chapter in Faith and Provision

Securing the part-time job at Yax Ciny Tailors was a small miracle for me at the time. After all the challenges I had been through, finally having some financial stability brought a sense of relief. It was a humble tailoring job, but to me, it meant so much more than just sewing clothes. It gave me confidence, taught me discipline, and provided for my basic needs. I was able to pay for my essential expenses, like food and transportation, and I could even contribute to EU activities whenever needed.

But balancing life was far from easy. As a student of English Literature, there was no shortage of academic demands. I had to keep up with reading assignments, essays, and exams. Yet my commitment to the Evangelical Union (EU) was just as significant, and I refused to neglect the spiritual growth I was experiencing. On top of this, the job at Yax Ciny Tailors required attention and skill. Life was busy— very busy—but in those moments of pressure, I learned to manage time with an almost mechanical precision.

I often joke now that I became a "time management machine" during this season. My days were packed, and every minute seemed like a precious resource I couldn't afford to waste. From the moment I woke up early in the morning to spend time in prayer and Bible study, to the late hours of tailoring work in the evening, each hour was accounted for. Yet, through it all, I never missed a college class, never skipped a single spiritual activity with the EU, and I was never absent from work at the shop. Looking back, I'm amazed at how God sustained me through such an intense period of my life. It was truly His grace that gave me the strength and focus to balance everything.

5.1 Spiritual Formation in Tenali (1993-1996)

Between 1993 and 1996, I went through a period of intense spiritual formation. My hunger for the Word of God grew stronger with each passing day. I found myself drawn to Scripture, eagerly reading and meditating on it at every opportunity. The Bible became my refuge, my source of strength. I started to see life through its lens, and it empowered me in ways I hadn't thought possible.

Fasting and prayer also became central to my spiritual journey during this time. There were days when I would fast and spend hours in prayer, seeking God's guidance and strength. The quiet moments of fasting drew me closer to God, and I began to experience deeper revelations of His will. Fasting was not just about abstaining from food; it was about submitting myself entirely to the Lord, trusting Him to fill the voids in my life with His presence.

I believe it was this spiritual hunger that prepared me for greater responsibilities in the

Evangelical Union. In 1994, the Lord opened the door for me to serve as the Prayer Secretary of Tenali EU. This was a pivotal moment for me, as I stepped into a role that required me to lead others in prayer. The weight of this responsibility was heavy, but it was also a time of tremendous growth. As the Prayer Secretary, I had to model the kind of prayer life I was encouraging others to cultivate. I took this role seriously and began to explore new ways to intercede for the lost, to pray for revival, and to stand in the gap for my fellow students.

5.2 Power of Early Morning Devotion

One of the most impactful lessons I learned during this season was the importance of praying for perishing souls. I would often rise before dawn, at times when the world was still asleep, and spend time interceding for those who didn't know Christ. I felt a deep burden for the lost, and this burden drove me to my knees, crying out to God for their salvation. I would also send prayer letters, asking for support from others to join me in this mission of prayer.

It was a quiet and humbling task, but one that I knew had eternal significance. The early morning hours became sacred to me. The silence of those moments allowed me to hear God's voice more clearly, and it was during these times that I received direction for my life and ministry. I could feel God stirring my heart, calling me to step into deeper waters of faith. Those early mornings weren't just about prayer; they were about preparation for the future that God was slowly unfolding before me.

The Need for a New Place for Ministry and Prayer

While my personal spiritual life was flourishing, I began to face practical challenges with my ministry work. Conducting Bible studies and prayer meetings in my hostel room at Ambedkar College became increasingly difficult. The room was small and offered little privacy, and as more students joined the EU, space became a significant issue.

That's when the idea of renting a separate house for ministry and prayer began to take shape. At first, the idea seemed far-fetched. I didn't have the resources to afford a place of my own, but I felt God was calling me to step out in faith. As I continued to pray, I felt a strong conviction that we needed a house with at least four rooms—enough space to accommodate Bible studies, prayer meetings, and even overnight stays for students involved in EU activities.

I knew this was going to be a challenge, but I also knew that with God, all things are possible. I started discussing the idea with a few other like-minded students in the hostel. To my surprise, two of them had been feeling the same burden. Together, we set out to find a house that could serve as our spiritual headquarters in Tenali.

The Search for a Prayer House

Finding the right house was not easy. We needed a place that was affordable, independent, and had enough space to meet our needs. Ideally, it would be close to Ambedkar College, so it would be convenient for students to come for prayer and Bible studies. We began searching in the nearby locality of Chinaravuru, a quiet area not far from the college.

House after house, we were met with rejection. Many landlords were wary of renting to us because of our faith. Some outright refused, afraid that our Christian gatherings might bring unwanted attention or conflict with their own beliefs. Others were willing but demanded rents far beyond what we could afford.

There were moments when we felt discouraged, but we never gave up. We believed that God had a specific place prepared for us, and we were determined to find it.

5.3 The Mysterious House on a Quiet Street

One evening, as I was walking down a narrow street in Chinaravuru, I stumbled upon a large, independent house. It was surrounded by a compound wall and had several coconut trees in the yard. The house looked abandoned, and the gate was locked. Something about the house caught my attention, and I felt a strong sense that this was the place God had prepared for us.

When I asked the neighbors about the house, I was met with a strange response. They called it the "devil's house" and warned me to stay away. They told me that two people had died in the house, and the owner had moved out because of a severe illness. According to them, the house had been cursed, and no one had lived there for years. They advised me to forget about it and look elsewhere, but I couldn't shake the feeling that this was the house God wanted us to have.

Facing the Fear and Pursuing the Vision

Despite the warnings, I decided to track down the owner. After some effort, I found him and learned more about the house's history. His two grown children had tragically died, and he was suffering from a serious kidney illness. He had locked the house and moved away, fearing that the tragedies would continue. But I believed that God would redeem this place for His purposes. I explained our vision for the house, and to my amazement, he agreed to rent it to us for a very low price. The rent was just Rs. 30, and my share was only Rs. 10, which was almost nothing.

I knew this was a miraculous provision from God. We moved in and began transforming the house into a place of prayer and ministry. It wasn't easy at first. The house had been emptied for so long that it felt dark and unwelcoming. But we believed that God's presence would fill the place and drive out any darkness.

The Transformation of the "Devil's House"

Our faith was soon rewarded. The house in Chinaravuru became a spiritual powerhouse. We held daily prayer meetings, singing sessions, and even all-night prayers. What had once been called the "devil's house" was now a place where the light of God's love and power shone brightly. Neighbors who had once feared the house began to notice the change. They saw students coming and going, singing praises to God, and praying fervently. The darkness that had once gripped the house was replaced by the warmth of God's presence.

I remember one night in particular when we experienced a strange incident. The three of us who lived in the house had gone to bed after a long day of ministry. In the middle of the night, I was awakened by the sound of something falling. When I opened my eyes, I saw a coconut oil bottle lying on my stomach. The bottle had somehow moved from a shelf on the other side of the room and landed on me. I knew this was the enemy trying to scare us, but instead of being afraid, I laughed. I saw it as a reminder that no matter how the enemy tried to attack us, God's power was greater.

We continued to hold all-night prayer meetings in the house, and soon, students from the college hostel began joining us. The house became known as a place of refuge, a place where people could encounter God in a deep and personal way. What started as a small group of believers grew into a vibrant community of students, all seeking God's face and longing for His presence.

Reflecting on God's Faithfulness

Looking back on my time in Tenali, I'm overwhelmed by God's faithfulness. He provided for every need, both practical and spiritual. He opened doors when it seemed like there were none, and He turned what others called a cursed house into a place of His glory. Those years in Tenali shaped me in ways I'm still discovering today. It was there that my faith deepened, and I learned to trust God in every aspect of my life. The lessons I learned during that time continue to influence my ministry and walk with God today.

A Legacy of Prayer and Faith

The house in Chinaravuru remains a testament to the power of prayer and faith. What began as a simple desire to find a place for ministry turned into a movement of God's Spirit that touched countless lives. Today, as I reflect on my EU journey, I'm reminded that God can use anyone, anywhere, to accomplish His purposes. All He requires is a willing heart and a life surrendered to His will.

In 1995, my life took another significant turn when I was entrusted with the role of president of the Evangelical Union (EU) in Tenali. I remember the day I was elected as president vividly—it felt like both a blessing and a burden. God had chosen me for this role, and I could feel His hand guiding me into leadership, but I knew this position would require a deeper level of commitment and spiritual maturity. My journey through the EU had already taught me many lessons, but this was going to be a time of even more intense learning.

5.4 Stepping into Leadership

Becoming the president of the EU was not just an honor; it was a spiritual challenge. I had never considered myself a leader before. I was still that same boy who had come to Tenali with nothing but a strong desire to know God and pursue my studies. I felt inadequate at first. Could I lead other students in their walk with God? Could I be a spiritual mentor when I was still learning so much myself?

But then, I remembered how the Lord had brought me through so many difficult situations already—my father's abandonment, the financial struggles, and the loneliness. Every challenge had been a stepping stone in preparing me for this role. My faith was being tested and strengthened. This new role required me to learn how to inspire others, how to teach the Word, and how to carry the burdens of those around me. But the Lord provided me with the courage to step forward.

My responsibilities increased, but so did my reliance on God. Balancing my academic life, my work at the tailoring shop, and my new leadership role was no small feat. Time management became crucial. I had to organize prayer meetings, Bible studies, and outreach programs while still maintaining my academic standing in college. There were moments of exhaustion, but every time I felt weak, God would lift me up. His strength was made perfect in my weakness.

The Support of EGF Members

One of the greatest blessings during this time was the community that formed around me. I was not alone in this journey. I had the privilege of working alongside passionate and committed students and graduates who supported me. People like Mr.

Prabhudas, Mrs. Gowri Kumari, Mr. Sudhakar Mondithoka, Mrs. Santha Kumari, Mr. Mark, Mr. Yesaiah, Dr. Rathnapradash, Mr. Ravi, Mr. Sudheer, Mrs. Manjari, Mrs. Manjulatha and several other professionals who belonged to EGF were pillars of strength in my life. Their presence was a constant reminder that God provides spiritual family even when our earthly family is absent or distant.

I recall one occasion when I was severely sick. It was during a time of intense ministry work, and I had been pushing myself too hard. The exhaustion took a toll on my health, and I developed terrible gastric ulcers. I was in pain and didn't know what to do. That's when Mr. Sudhakar stepped in. He took me to the railway hospital and stayed by my side. His care and concern reminded me of a father's love, something I had missed deeply since my own father couldn't offer.

Another time, when I was struggling again with health issues, Mr. Prabhudas came to my room and took me to a doctor. He paid the doctor's fees and ensured I had the necessary medicines. His actions were a reflection of Christ's love—caring for the needy and standing with those who are weak. These men showed me what it meant to be part of a spiritual family. They did not just preach about love; they lived it out in their actions.

During my time as president of the Tenali EU, Mrs. Santha Kumari stood out as a guiding presence in my spiritual journey. As a senior adviser to the EU, she not only provided invaluable spiritual counsel but also extended a motherly love and care that deeply impacted my life. Her open home ministry became a refuge for my weary soul during moments of struggle and uncertainty. Her gentle wisdom and nurturing spirit were instrumental in helping me navigate the complexities of leadership and spiritual growth during that season of my life.

Her home was always open, not just as a physical place but as a sanctuary where I found warmth, encouragement, and direction. She cared for me as if I were her own child, providing a sense of family that I often lacked during those challenging years. Her prayers, insightful advice, and the atmosphere of her home gave me renewed strength to carry on the work God had entrusted to me in the EU.

Through her ministry, I learned the power of

hospitality in advancing God's kingdom. Mrs. Kumari's willingness to offer her time, resources, and love reflected the heart of Christ in a way that left a lasting imprint on my life. Her influence extended far beyond meetings and programs—she modeled a life of faith, service, and unconditional love, which I have carried with me ever since.

The Power of Christian Homes

The homes of these graduates were open to me and other students like me. Their hospitality was a balm to my weary soul. After spending days juggling studies, work, and ministry, their homes became places of refuge where I could rest and be refreshed. I can never forget how these homes reflected the love of Christ. They were not just physical places; they were spiritual havens where I experienced the warmth and comfort of Christian fellowship.

Each time I stepped into their homes, I was treated like a member of their own family. The meals they shared, the conversations we had, and the prayers we offered together gave me strength. They taught me what a Christian home should look like—a place of love, respect, and open arms for ministry. These families embodied the heart of God's people, and I learned so much from watching their lives.

In these homes, I saw the value of finding God's will in marriage, respecting a spouse, and creating an environment that nurtures faith. The couples in these homes were examples of how-to walk-in unity, serving God together. Their marriages were built on Christ, and I learned valuable lessons on how to live out a God-centered relationship, lessons that would serve me well later in life.

Mr. Prabhudas and Mrs. Gowri Kumari played a significant role in my spiritual journey during my time as a student of the Tenali EU. Their home was a place where I felt the warmth of family and experienced love, care, and support in an extraordinary way. Mrs. Gowri Kumari, a dedicated lecturer at JMJ College, Tenali, balanced her professional life with a deep commitment to nurturing the young people of the EU. They welcomed me into their home, offering not just physical hospitality but also emotional and spiritual nourishment.

Their open home ministry provided a space where I could find respite from the pressures of leadership and the struggles I faced at that time. Mrs. Gowri Kumari and Mr. Prabhudas treated me like a family member, offering wise counsel and encouragement whenever I needed it. They became a source of strength and guidance, their home a sanctuary of peace where I could reflect, recharge, and refocus on God's purpose for my life. It was in their home that I witnessed the beauty of Christian fellowship lived out in everyday life.

What stood out most was their unwavering commitment to supporting my spiritual journey. Whether it was through a quiet conversation over a meal, a heartfelt prayer, or simply their presence in times of need, the love and care they extended as a family went beyond words. Their open home was not just a refuge for me but for many others, embodying the heart of Christ through their generosity and compassion. The impact of their ministry during that season of my life is something I will always cherish, as it profoundly shaped my understanding of godly family life and hospitality.

Leading with Fire and Passion

As president of the EU, I had the responsibility

of organizing not just prayer meetings, but also outreach efforts. One particular outreach event stands out in my memory. We organized an all-night prayer vigil, which became a turning point for many of the students. God's presence was so powerful that night, and I could see how the Holy Spirit was working in the hearts of the young men gathered there. It wasn't just about the prayers we offered; it was about the deep repentance, the revival of faith, and the commitment to follow Jesus more closely.

I remember one of my classmates, who had been struggling with sin and guilt for a long time, coming up to me in tears after the vigil. He was convicted of his sin and wanted to repent. He pulled me aside and began weeping, confessing the things that had been holding him back. It was a moment of breakthrough for him, and I saw firsthand the power of prayer and repentance. These kinds of experiences fueled my passion for ministry. I knew that God was using me in ways I could not have imagined.

Through these experiences, I realized that leadership in the Kingdom of God was not about power or prestige. It was about serving others, lifting them up, and helping them grow in their faith. It was about humility, compassion, and a willingness to stand with others in their struggles. I was learning how to lead with fire, but it was a fire kindled by the Holy Spirit, not by human ambition.

Facing Challenges with Confidence

Of course, the path wasn't always easy. There were moments of doubt and fear, times when I wondered if I was truly capable of handling the responsibilities placed on my shoulders. Financial struggles continued to be a constant pressure. Although my part-time job at Yax Ciny Tailors gave me some stability, it was never enough to cover all my expenses. There were days when I didn't know how I would make it through the week, but every time, God provided.

I learned to trust God in ways I had never imagined. One of the key lessons I learned during this period was that God's provision often comes in unexpected ways. Whether it was through the generosity of others, a surprise gift, or a part-time job opportunity, God always made a way. These experiences taught me the true meaning of faith. Faith was not just believing in God's existence; it was trusting Him for every need, no matter how small or how great.

Looking back now, I see how those years of poverty and struggle were shaping me. They were preparing me for the greater challenges I would face in life and ministry. I learned perseverance, patience, and above all, trust in God's timing. Every setback was an opportunity to grow deeper in faith and to rely more fully on the Lord.

As I reflect on my time as president of the Tenali EU, I am filled with gratitude. Gratitude for the people who walked alongside me, for the lessons I learned, and for the ways God used me despite my weaknesses. Those years were foundational for my spiritual growth, and I will always treasure the memories of that time.

The journey wasn't easy, but it was worth every struggle. God was molding me into a leader, not just for the EU but for the future work He had prepared for me. I came to understand that leadership is not about having all the answers or being the strongest person in the room. Leadership is about being willing to serve, to love, and to trust God with everything.

The students and graduates of Tenali EU will always hold a special place in my heart. Their love, support, and encouragement carried me through some of the most challenging years of my life. Through them, God showed me that even when we feel alone, we are never truly alone in His family. Their impact on my life is immeasurable, and I will always be grateful for their role in my spiritual journey.

A Step of Faith and Baptism

As I grew spiritually during my time with the Tenali Evangelical Union (EU), my heart yearned for a deeper commitment to the Almighty God. I began to understand that baptism was not merely a ritual but a public declaration of my faith, an outward testimony of the inward transformation that had already taken place in my soul. On the 1st of January, 1994, I took this important step of obedience. The place was Beracha Baktsingh Church in Tenali, a sacred sanctuary where I had found spiritual nurturing. There, in the presence of fellow believers, I declared my allegiance to the Lord through water baptism. That day marked a pivotal moment in my walk with Christ—a profound step that solidified my commitment to the Lord's calling.

The experience was life-changing, not because of the ceremony itself but because of the sense of renewal and clarity that accompanied it. It was as though my past burdens had been washed away in the waters of baptism, and I emerged with a new sense of purpose and peace. This act of obedience was a symbol of my spiritual resurrection, of leaving behind the old and stepping into the new. I felt my life, once filled with doubts and uncertainties, was now being directed by the Almighty God Himself.

6. The Call to Ministry

Only a few weeks after my baptism, on the 26th of January, 1994, I attended a retreat. It was during this retreat that I distinctly sensed the Lord's calling for full-time ministry. The retreat was a time of reflection and seeking God's will, and as I spent time in prayer, the voice of the Lord became unmistakably clear. It was as though the Almighty Himself had placed a burden on my heart to serve Him in a deeper capacity, beyond the walls of ordinary life, and to dedicate myself wholly to His mission.

Initially, I was overwhelmed. What did this mean for my life? Could I really walk the path of full-time ministry when I had so many uncertainties about my future? The Lord, however, did not leave me in doubt. Over the following weeks and months, He confirmed this call in numerous ways. Every sermon I heard, every scripture I read, every conversation I had pointed me back to this one undeniable truth—I was called to serve the Lord fully, without reservation.

There were moments when I wrestled with the enormity of this calling. The idea of leaving behind the security of a conventional career path and stepping into the unknown was daunting. Yet, every time I brought my fears and concerns before the Lord, He reassured me with His peace. The more I prayed, the clearer my direction became. This was not just a fleeting emotional experience—it was a divine commission, and I could no longer ignore it.

Leadership in Missions

Shortly after I embraced the call to ministry, the Lord provided me with an opportunity that would shape my leadership abilities. I was invited to join the

Missions Department of UESI-AP (Union of Evangelical Studetns of India - Andhra Pradesh) as a student member. This responsibility was more than an honor—it was a divine appointment that would not only empower me but also open new doors for ministry. As a student, I was entrusted with leadership roles that required both wisdom and humility. I found myself organizing prayer meetings, coordinating mission events, and encouraging my peers to engage in mission work.

This experience was transformative. I began to see missions not just as an activity but as a lifestyle, a calling that required my full attention. Leading prayer cells and organizing mission-focused activities stirred in me a passion for the lost and the unreached. I felt the weight of the Great Commission in a way I had never felt before. The responsibility of leading others in prayer for missions gave me a glimpse into the broader work of the Kingdom, and I began to understand the vital role that prayer played in advancing the gospel.

Missions became my passion. I was no longer content with merely attending church or participating in EU activities—I wanted to be on the frontlines of the

Lord's work. Whether it was organizing a small prayer meeting or speaking at a missions conference, I knew that this was where the Lord was leading me. The fire for missions burned deep within me, and I longed to see lives transformed by the power of the gospel.

The Path Forward

As I approached the completion of my BA in English Literature, my heart was full of anticipation for the next step. The Lord had already placed a burden for full-time ministry on my heart, but I needed further direction and confirmation. I was at a crossroads, with one foot in the world of academics and the other in the world of ministry. My education was important, but it was clear to me that the Lord had something greater in store. I often found myself praying for guidance, asking the Lord to make His will known with greater clarity.

During this season of transition, I wrestled with many questions. How would my family respond to my decision to enter full-time ministry? Would they understand? Would they support me? At that time, none of my family members were walking with me on this spiritual journey. They did not share the same convictions, and this created a sense of isolation. I feared that choosing ministry might alienate me further from those I loved.

Yet, amid these doubts, I remained confident in the Lord's faithfulness. I knew that if He had called me, He would also provide the grace and courage I needed to take each step forward. The journey was not going to be easy, but I trusted that the Lord would continue to lead and guide me.

A Cry for Confirmation

Although I had sensed the Lord's calling and had experienced His provision in opening doors for leadership and missions, there remained a lingering desire in my heart for further confirmation. I wanted to be absolutely certain that this was the path the Lord had chosen for me. I sought more conviction from the Almighty—clear, undeniable signs that this was His perfect will.

In my times of prayer, I laid this burden before the Lord. I asked Him to confirm His calling, not just through external signs but through an inner peace that surpassed all understanding. I knew that if this was truly the path I was meant to take, the Lord would remove all doubt and replace it with unwavering confidence.

I continued to grow in His grace, trusting that the Lord would provide clarity in His perfect timing. I didn't know what the future held, but I was learning to trust the One who held the future. I knew that as I continued to seek His will and walk in obedience, the rest of the story would unfold according to His divine plan.

6.1 Summer of 1996 – A Time of Seeking

As the summer of 1996 unfolded, I found myself at a pivotal juncture in my life. My BA in English Literature was now complete, and I was left with a looming question: What next? The time had come to take the next step, but which direction was I supposed to go? My heart had long been stirred by a desire to serve God in full-time ministry, but doubts still lingered. How could I be sure this was truly God's will for my life?

I reflected on my journey so far—the many moments where God had clearly been at work, the personal encounters with His presence, and the passion that had grown within me for missions and spiritual leadership. But despite these experiences, I found myself yearning for more—a deeper confirmation, a clearer sign from God that full-time ministry was not just a desire of my heart but a calling He had placed upon me.

My family, while supportive of my academic pursuits, did not share the spiritual journey I was on. This distance left me feeling somewhat isolated, and with that came uncertainty. Could I really embark on such a path without the full understanding and backing of those closest to me? How would I provide for myself? How would I answer the inevitable questions that would arise about my future? These questions weighed heavily on me, and they kept me from moving forward with confidence.

It was in this moment of uncertainty that I turned to God with greater intensity. I knew I needed more than just inner conviction—I needed an encounter with Him. I needed to hear His voice clearly, to receive an unmistakable confirmation that would settle the doubts that clouded my mind.

So, I did what I knew best—I turned to fasting and prayer.

Fasting, Prayer, and the Desire for Confirmation

During this period of seeking, I entered into a time of focused fasting and prayer. For days, I withdrew from the usual activities of life, dedicating my time solely to hearing from God. I had long believed that fasting had the power to break spiritual barriers, and this time was no different. I was desperate to encounter the Lord, to receive a confirmation that would affirm my calling to full-time ministry.

The time spent in prayer was profound. I could feel God's presence drawing closer as I sought Him earnestly. My heart was in a state of vulnerability, open to whatever He would reveal to me. Yet, as the days passed, I found myself still longing for a specific word, a sign that would confirm my calling beyond any shadow of a doubt.

Despite the rich moments of communion with God during this time, I remained unsettled. While I felt the Lord's presence, I still needed a defining moment that would remove all uncertainty. And so, I continued to seek Him with all my heart, trusting that He would provide the clarity I needed in His time.

6.2 Leadership Training Camp at Gunadala

It was during this intense season of prayer and

fasting that an opportunity arose for me to lead a Leadership Training Camp. The camp was held at Joseph's English Medium High School in Gunadala, Vijayawada. As the president of the EU, it was my responsibility to oversee the camp, ensuring that the students who attended would leave equipped for leadership and spiritual growth.

While organizing and directing the camp required a great deal of focus and energy, my mind was still preoccupied with one singular purpose: hearing from God. I entered the camp with an open heart, expecting that amidst the teachings and devotions, the Lord would speak to me and provide the confirmation I sought.

The camp was a rich time of fellowship and learning. We gathered daily for sessions on leadership, ministry, and spiritual development. I took great joy in mentoring the students and seeing their passion for Christ grow. But for me personally, the camp held an even deeper significance—I believed that this would be the place where I would encounter God in a fresh way.

The evening devotions, in particular, became a time of deep reflection. Each night, after the day's sessions were over, we would gather for a time of worship and teaching. It was during these moments, with hearts open and spirits receptive, that I sensed the Lord drawing near.

The Lord's Voice in the Camp

One evening, the guest speaker for the camp, Dr. John Paul, delivered a powerful message on the life and mission of Moses. He preached with great conviction, recounting the story of Moses' encounter with God at the burning bush. Dr. John Paul emphasized how Moses, despite his many hesitations and feelings of inadequacy, was called by God to lead the Israelites out of Egypt. He spoke of how God had chosen Moses not because of his qualifications but because of his willingness to respond to the divine call.

As I sat there, listening to Dr. John Paul speak, something stirred within me. The story of Moses seemed to mirror my own journey—the questions, the doubts, the desire for confirmation. Moses had hesitated when God called him, unsure of how he could possibly fulfill such a monumental task. And yet, God had reassured him, promising to be with him every step of the way.

Dr. John Paul's words resonated deeply in my heart. It was as if he was speaking directly to me, addressing the very struggles I had been facing. His message cut through the doubts that had clouded my mind, and for the first time in a long while, I felt a sense of peace beginning to take hold.

I realized that just as God had called Moses, despite his weaknesses and hesitations, He was calling me too. God wasn't looking for perfection—He was looking for a willing heart. And though I still had questions about how everything would unfold, I began to understand that it wasn't about having all the answers. It was about trusting in the God who calls.

The message that evening was a turning point. As I left the session and reflected on Dr. John Paul's sermon, I felt a deep sense of assurance settling in my spirit. Many of the doubts I had carried were beginning to lift. However, though I felt encouraged, I knew that I wasn't completely convinced yet. There were still questions I needed answered, and I longed for a deeper, more personal confirmation.

Little did I know, the Lord had something extraordinary in store for me—a divine encounter that would remove any remaining doubt and set my feet firmly on the path He had laid out for me.

6.3 A Divine Encounter: Walking by Faith to Tenali"

Even though the Lord spoke to me clearly during the camp, something inside me still wrestled with doubts. I longed for a divine encounter, a tangible moment where God's voice would not only comfort me but also confirm the call He had placed on my life. It was the final day of the camp, and I was preparing to return to Tenali. As I packed my bags, my heart was still heavy. I prayed earnestly, seeking the Lord's guidance.

Suddenly, the Lord whispered to my heart: *"Walk to Tenali by foot, and I will show you my glory."* At first, I thought it was an illusion. How could this be God speaking? Walking nearly 30 kilometers on foot in the heat of May seemed impossible. Yet, His voice persisted, and I knew I had to obey, for as it is written: *"Trust in the Lord with all your heart and lean not on your own understanding; in all your ways submit to him, and he will make your paths straight" (Proverbs 3:5-6).*

I decided to give my bag to Tirupathi Rao, the

student leader I had been training to succeed me as president of the Evangelical Union (EU). I asked him to travel back with the rest of the group, while I prepared to take this unusual journey alone. It was around 6 p.m. when I stepped outside the school building, intending to begin my walk. However, I saw a group of students gathered near the bus stop. I knew if they saw me, they would insist that I join them on the bus, so I decided to take a different path.

Climbing Gunadala Hill

Instead of walking through the streets of Vijayawada, I took a path that led me to the top of Gunadala Hill. This hill, known for its Catholic shrine, offered a panoramic view of the city. By the time I reached the top, the sun had already set, and darkness had fallen. The only sounds I could hear were the rustling of leaves and the distant hum of city life. From the hilltop, I could see people below walking and driving their motorcycles like ants scurrying about. At that moment, the Holy Spirit whispered to me: *"Who will share my love with these perishing souls?"*

Moved by the voice of God, I knelt down on the hill and surrendered myself once again to His will, saying, *"Here am I. Send me!"* (Isaiah 6:8). The Lord's call to serve Him had never been clearer, and I felt His presence overwhelming me with a sense of peace and purpose.

The Start of a Long Journey

After spending some time in prayer, I descended the hill from the other side, far from the direction of Tenali. Since I had given my money and bag to Tirupathi Rao, I had nothing with me but the clothes I wore. The Lord reminded me that I was to walk this journey as a demonstration of faith, and He would provide for me along the way. *"My grace is sufficient for you, for my power is made perfect in weakness" (2 Corinthians 12:9),* He assured me.

With only a pair of rubber slippers that were ill-suited for such a long walk, I began my journey towards Tenali. The heat of Vijayawada in late May was brutal. Anyone who has experienced the summer in Andhra Pradesh knows that the temperatures can be unbearable. The fourth week of May is known as *Rohinikarthi* in the Telugu language—a time when even the locals dare not venture out in the sweltering sun. Yet, God had called me to walk this path, and I trusted that He would sustain me.

As I walked towards Prakasham Barrage, I began to feel the weight of my physical exhaustion. I had been fasting for several days, and my body was weak from hunger. By the time I crossed the barrage, it was 9:30 p.m., and I was utterly spent. I found a cement pole belonging to a political party flag and collapsed beside it, unable to go any further. I drifted into a deep sleep right there on the roadside, without any comfort or shelter.

Awakening to a New Challenge

When I opened my eyes, it was early morning—around 6 a.m.—and the traffic had already begun to move. I felt sick and fatigued but knew I had to continue walking. *"Even youths grow tired and weary, and young men stumble and fall, but those who hope in the Lord will renew their strength" (Isaiah 40:30-31).* I leaned on this promise as I made my way towards Mangalagiri, a small town between Vijayawada and Tenali.

Though it was still morning, the heat waves began to beat down on me by 7 a.m. The sun was relentless, and my body began to suffer from sunstroke.

I became dehydrated and started experiencing loose motions, which further drained my energy. I could feel my strength fading with every step, yet the Lord spoke to me, *"This journey is like your full-time ministry. It will be difficult, but my presence will always be with you."* This word from the Lord was a comfort, reminding me that even in hardship, He would sustain me. *"The Lord is my shepherd; I shall not want. He makes me lie down in green pastures. He leads me beside still waters. He restores my soul"* *(Psalm 23:1-3).*

Seeking Refuge in Mangalagiri

By the time I reached Mangalagiri, it was almost noon. The sun was directly overhead, and the temperature had soared. I felt as if my body was burning from both the heat of the road beneath my feet and the blazing sun above. My rubber slippers had torn apart, and I was now walking barefoot on the scalding tar. As I walked through the fields, my motions became uncontrollable again, and my body was on the verge of collapse.

In this moment of weakness, I remembered that Pastor Millington, who had baptized me in Tenali, had been transferred to Mangalagiri. I decided to seek him out, hoping to find some comfort and assistance. When I arrived at the church, Pastor Millington recognized me immediately. He asked me how I had arrived in such a state, and I explained the journey God had sent me on. I told him about my desire to enter full-time ministry and my need for a baptism certificate, as my Hindu name might cause others to doubt my faith.

The pastor welcomed me with open arms, offering me tea—my first food in three days. His kindness was a reminder of God's provision, for *"the Lord will provide for all your needs according to the riches of his glory in Christ Jesus" (Philippians 4:19).* He blessed me, gave me the certificate I needed, and sent me on my way.

The Final Leg: A Divine Encounter

It was 2 p.m. by the time I left Mangalagiri, and the heat had become unbearable. My feet, now bare, were blistering from the hot tar, and the heat waves from the sun felt like they were crushing me. I moved off the road and began walking through the fields, but even here, I found no relief. The combination of dehydration, loose motions, and exhaustion took its toll, and by the time I reached Duggirala—a small town close to Tenali—I could barely stand.

As I walked through the empty paddy fields, I felt my body giving up. There were no people around, and the isolation added to my despair. I stumbled, falling into unconsciousness under the scorching sun. I lay there for nearly an hour, lost to the world when I felt something cool on my cheeks. It was water. As I opened my eyes, I saw a man dressed in white, like an angel, pouring water into my mouth from a huge jug.

Could this be an angel of the Lord? I wondered. The water was unlike anything I had ever tasted—it was sweet, like coconut water, and as it filled my body, I felt my strength returning. My muscles, which had been weak and frail, were now full of power. I felt as if I had the strength of a thousand elephants.

The man smiled at me, touched my shoulder, and said, *"You can go now. You will be all right."* As quickly as he had appeared, he disappeared. I knew, without a doubt, that this was a divine encounter. The Lord had sent an angel to revive me, and in that moment, I felt God's overwhelming love and assurance. *"For he will command his angels concerning you to guard you in all your ways" (Psalm 91:11).*

Confirmation of the Call

I continued my journey to Tenali, and when I finally arrived at my room, I collapsed on my bed, utterly spent but full of peace. As I lay there, the Lord spoke to me again: *"Get up and go. It was I who saved you with my angel, and I will never leave you. This journey is your full-time mission. It will be tough, but I will be with you."* This encounter with God in such a dramatic and personal way confirmed my calling, and from that day forward, I never doubted His plan for my life. *"I can do all things through Christ who strengthens me" (Philippians 4:13).*

6.4 Packing My Bags for Ministry: A Leap of Faith
"For we live by faith, not by sight." (2 Corinthians 5:7)

Returning from my transformative journey to Tenali, I felt as though I had crossed a spiritual threshold. The divine interventions I had experienced during my walk from Vijayawada to Tenali were a confirmation of the Lord's call upon my life. His miraculous provision and angelic presence reaffirmed my decision to serve Him fully. However, as I returned to my humble room and looked at my belongings, I realized that I had no clear direction. Where would I go? How would I begin this journey of full-time ministry? These questions loomed large in my heart. The assurance of God's presence was my only certainty.

That night, as I lay awake pondering the next step, a name flashed in my mind—Mr. Arul Selva Raj. He had once invited me to come to Hyderabad for some mission exposure through a post card. Suddenly, it seemed as though the Holy Spirit was reminding me of this conversation. Could this be where God wanted me to go next? As it says in *Proverbs 16:9*, *"In their hearts, humans plan their course, but the Lord establishes their steps."* With no other leads, I decided to pursue this faint direction with faith.

Disposing of Everything: A Heart Set on God

"Do not store up for yourselves treasures on earth, where moths and vermin destroy, and where thieves break in and steal. But store up for yourselves treasures in heaven." (Matthew 6:19-20)

The next morning, with conviction filling my heart, I began packing my few belongings. The room that had been my sanctuary for some time now seemed like a memory from the past. I knew that to fully embrace this new call, I had to leave behind everything that held me back, including the books I had gathered during my years in Tenali. They had been a source of knowledge and comfort, but I realized that I would need to travel light for the mission ahead. I disposed of nearly everything except for an extra pair of clothes, which I packed in a simple sackcloth bag.

My financial situation was dire. I had been without work for a month and possessed only Rs.50 in my pocket. I used this small sum to buy an ordinary train ticket from Tenali to Secunderabad. As I held that ticket in my hand, I felt a mix of emotions—uncertainty, excitement, and a deep sense of reliance on God. It was as though God was teaching me the lesson of the manna from heaven: He would provide for my daily needs, one day at a time. *"And my God will meet all your needs according to the riches of his glory in Christ Jesus." (Philippians 4:19)*

A Train Ride of Questions

"Cast all your anxiety on him because he cares for you." (1 Peter 5:7)

As I boarded the train and found a seat, a wave of questions flooded my mind. Where was this journey going to end? What would I do when I reached Hyderabad? What if Mr. Arul wasn't available or couldn't help? These questions swirled, but deep within, I had a profound sense of peace. The God who had guided me so far would not abandon me now. The journey on the Repalle to Secunderabad passenger train was long and slow, giving me ample time to reflect. I felt like Abraham, leaving his homeland without knowing where God was leading him. *"By faith, Abraham obeyed when he was called to go out to a place that he was to receive as an inheritance. He went out, not knowing where he was going." (Hebrews 11:8)*

As the train moved through the villages and fields, I prayed continuously, committing my future to God's hands. I knew this was not just a physical journey but a spiritual one, where I would learn to trust God in deeper ways. *"The Lord himself goes before you and will be with you; he will never leave you nor forsake you. Do not be afraid; do not be discouraged." (Deuteronomy 31:8)*

6.5 Arriving in Secunderabad: A City of

Uncertainty

"The Lord is my shepherd, I lack nothing." (Psalm 23:1)

When the train finally pulled into Secunderabad station, it was 7 p.m. The sun had set, and the bustling station was filled with travelers going about their business. I stepped onto the platform with nothing but my sackcloth bag, Rs.10 left in my pocket, and the address of Mr. Arul written on a postcard. I didn't have money to take an auto or a city bus, so I began to walk. I had no idea where the Tukaram Gate area was, but I trusted that God would guide me as He had before.

With every step, I prayed, asking the Lord for strength and direction. Eventually, I found a few people who could point me toward the general direction of Tukaram Gate. However, when I finally reached the address written on the postcard, my heart sank—the door was locked, and no one was home. I stood there in the fading light, unsure of what to do next. Secunderabad was a large and unfamiliar city, and I knew no one else there. But I clung to the promise that *"The Lord is near to all who call on him, to all who call on him in truth." (Psalm 145:18).*

A Night on the Streets: My First Mission in Hyderabad

"Even the sparrow has found a home, and the swallow a nest for herself, where she may have her young—a place near your altar, Lord Almighty." *(Psalm 84:3)*

With nowhere to go and no money for lodging, I wandered the streets until I found a small, open bus shed. It was exposed to the elements and far from comfortable, but I had no other option. That night, the bus shed became my makeshift home, and the mosquitoes, ants, and flies became my companions. Their bites were constant, and sleep was elusive, but as I lay there, I realized that this was my first night in ministry.

This experience brought me closer to God in ways I hadn't anticipated. *"For here we do not have an enduring city, but we are looking for the city that is to come."* *(Hebrews 13:14).* Despite the physical discomfort, I felt a profound sense of joy in knowing that I was walking the path God had called me to. The humility of that night reminded me of the Apostle Paul's words: *"I know what it is to be in need, and I know what it is to have plenty. I have learned the secret *of being content in any and every situation, whether well fed or hungry, whether living in plenty or in want." (Philippians 4:12).*

God's Provision in Unexpected Places

"And we know that in all things God works for the good of those who love him, who have been called according to his purpose." (Romans 8:28)

The next morning, after a restless night, I found Arul in his room. He welcomed me warmly into his room, offering me the hospitality and kindness I desperately needed. God had provided, just as He had promised. His roommates Prabhudanam and Apprao had been a great help to me during my stay with him in the room.

Arul introduced me to a man named Mr. S.P. Daniel, another Tamilian who had a deep heart for missions. He quickly took me under his wing, and through his connections, I was admitted to the Gospel for Asia Biblical Training Center at Bandalguda in Hyderabad. This was the beginning of a new chapter in my life, where God would mold and equip me for the ministry ahead. *"The Lord will guide you always; he will satisfy your needs in a sun-scorched land and will strengthen your frame. You will be like a well-watered garden, like a spring whose waters never fail." (Isaiah 58:11).*

6.6 Training at Gospel for Asia

I had just completed my Bachelor of Arts in English Literature when God opened an unexpected door for me at the Gospel for Asia (GFA) training center. It was a time when I felt both excitement and uncertainty. With nothing more than my faith and a deep desire to serve God, I entered the gates of this training center, not knowing how much of an impact it would have on my life and future. "For I know the plans I have for you, declares the Lord, plans for welfare and not for evil, to give you a future and a hope." (Jeremiah 29:11).

Looking back, I see how God's plans were unfolding for me in ways I could not comprehend at that time. GFA was not just a place of learning; it was a place of discipline, service, and immense personal growth. The intensity of the training felt similar to military discipline. The teachers at GFA, Mr. Jayarao, Mr. Danny, Mr. Jose PS, Mr. John Paul, Mr. Jasper, Mr. Muneer, and many others, were not only my instructors but also my mentors. They embodied the virtues of hard work, commitment, and unwavering faith in God. I am eternally grateful to God for them.

They taught us with passion and strictness, ensuring that we grew spiritually and became equipped for ministry. We were provided free education, lodging, and boarding, which was a great blessing. However, I had no pocket money to meet my basic needs. Most of the students came from families that could support them financially, but I had none to send me help.

I felt God's hand in all of this and trusted Him for my provision. Little did I know, God was preparing something special for me.

A Time of Testing and Translation

During this time, my proficiency in English, gained from my BA degree, became invaluable. Many of our teachers were from Kerala, and though they were fluent in English, they were unable to communicate effectively in Telugu, which was the native language of the students. This created a gap, and I was given the responsibility to bridge it by translating their teachings. This was both a challenge and a privilege. I translated during class hours, making the teachings accessible to my fellow students.

This opportunity not only helped me develop relationships with the teachers but also introduced me to new friendships with my fellow students. My loneliness began to dissipate as I formed bonds with those around me. I found a renewed sense of purpose in this role and was thankful for the friendships that were being built.

A Moment of Desperation

One day, however, I faced a test of a different kind. My extra pair of clothes had become dirty, and I had no soap to wash them. I didn't have any extra clothes to wear. All the other students received money from their parents or sponsors to meet such basic needs, but I had no one to send me any. My frustration grew. I felt helpless, and the weight of my financial struggles was too much to bear.

It was the 15th of August, 1996—India's Independence Day. The campus was alive with celebrations, and the kitchen had prepared a special Hyderabadi biryani for the students. However, I couldn't celebrate. I felt an inner turmoil and decided to retreat to a solitary place within the 30-acre campus. I knelt down among the bushes at 9 a.m., determined to pour out my heart to God. My spirit was broken, and I needed an answer. Time passed, but I remained on my knees, refusing to get up until the Lord responded. By 3 p.m., I was still praying, completely absorbed in my conversation with God.

"Call to me and I will answer you and tell you great and unsearchable things you do not know." (Jeremiah 33:3)

And then, I heard a gentle voice speak to me: "*Get up and go. I have prepared more than what you have asked me.*" Those words filled me with peace and confidence. I knew that God had heard my plea, and I got up from my knees, ready to walk in faith.

God's Provision Arrives

As I walked towards the college office, I saw Mr. Jayarao, one of my teachers and the speaker for the "Athmeeya Yathra" Telugu radio program, coming towards me. He had been looking for me. As we approached each other, he said, "I have been searching for you. I have good news for you; come and sit."

He told me that he had fought with the director,

Mr. Jose PS, to arrange a part-time job for me at the institute. From that day onward, I became his assistant, helping him with typing, preparing itineraries, and responding to letters from listeners of the radio program. For this, I would be paid Rs. 300 every month—a significant amount for me, more than enough to meet my basic needs.

"And my God will meet all your needs according to the riches of his glory in Christ Jesus." (Philippians 4:19)

This part-time job was more than just a provision of income. It was a direct answer to the prayer I had prayed that very morning. I was overwhelmed with gratitude, knowing that God had heard my cries and had answered in such a tangible way.

From that point onward, I became an essential part of the college. Every teacher sought my assistance, and I was constantly busy helping with various tasks, from translating during class hours to assisting SP Daniel in his ministry to the neighbors, and even running errands for the accountant at the institute. I felt God's favor upon me in everything I did. I wasn't just a student; I was serving in a place of influence and purpose.

A Time of Growth and Service

This period at GFA was a time of immense growth for me—spiritually, emotionally, and intellectually. It was a season marked by prayer, discipline, hard work, and sacrificial service. I was deeply invested in the mission and found joy in serving others. By the time I graduated in May 1996, I had not only completed my missionary training but had also earned the award for Best Student.

"Whatever you do, work heartily, as for the Lord and not for men, knowing that from the Lord you will receive the inheritance as your reward. You are serving the Lord Christ." (Colossians 3:23-24)

The experience at GFA was transformative. It was during this time that I realized the depth of God's calling on my life. I had entered the institute with dreams of becoming a missionary in a remote place, serving the unreached, but God was about to take me on a different journey.

Encouraged to Pursue Higher Education

My spiritual mentor, Mr. Jayarao, recognized

the potential in me. As I began to dream about my future in ministry, he advised me to pursue higher education. He encouraged me to apply for my Master of Divinity (M.Div) studies at the GFA seminary in Tiruvalla, Kerala. I remember his words clearly: "Venkat, you should go higher and higher, and you should become better than me in the mission of God."

"For wisdom is better than jewels, and all that you may desire cannot compare with her." (Proverbs 8:11)

His encouragement and selfless mentorship shaped my future in ways I could never have imagined. Despite his high position as a radio speaker, he remained humble and committed to discipling students like me. It was because of his unwavering belief in me that I continued my journey of higher education, trusting God every step of the way.

With my GFA training complete, I looked ahead to the next phase of my life in Kerala. Little did I know that the experiences awaiting me there would further shape my spiritual awakening and prepare me for the greater mission God had in store.

6.7 M.Div. Studies at GFA Seminary, Kerala

After completing my training at the Gospel for Asia (GFA) Center in Hyderabad, I faced a new challenge—how to continue my education at the seminary in Kerala for the Master of Divinity (M.Div) program. Though I had secured a seat, I didn't know how I would pay the tuition fees or survive in such a distant, unfamiliar place. My situation seemed impossible, yet God had consistently provided for me in the past. I held on to the truth of His provision, just as it says in Philippians 4:19, "And my God will meet all your needs according to the riches of his glory in Christ Jesus."

My only weapon during that time was fasting and prayer. I had no money to buy a train ticket, let alone support myself through three years of rigorous study. Time was running out as the M.Div program was set to begin in June, and I finished my training in Hyderabad by May. With only a month to go, I turned to God in complete dependence, fasting and praying for five days. I remember pouring out my heart to the Lord, reminding Him of His promises, and begging Him for a way forward.

On the fifth day of my fast, a Tamil sister—

whose name, unfortunately, has slipped from my memory—approached me and gave me Rs.1000 as a gift. She didn't know my needs, but God did. That amount was exactly what I needed to book my train ticket to Kerala and have some pocket money to start my new life at the seminary. I was overwhelmed with gratitude. It was a reminder that God, who sees our struggles and hears our prayers, is always faithful. I thought of Psalm 37:25, "I was young and now I am old, yet I have never seen the righteous forsaken or their children begging bread."

With my train ticket purchased and enough funds to get me started, I set off for Kerala, trusting that God had already gone before me to make the crooked paths straight. As the train carried me closer to my destination, I marveled at the journey God had taken me on. Each step, He had provided, sometimes at the very last moment, but always right on time.

The Beauty of Kerala and GFA Seminary

Kerala, the "God's Own Country," greeted me with its lush greenery, coconut groves, and serene backwaters. The state's natural beauty was overwhelming—a stark contrast to the arid regions I had been accustomed to. Tiruvalla, where GFA's seminary was located, was no exception. It felt like I had stepped into a peaceful, divine oasis.

The GFA seminary itself was even more impressive. The campus was well-equipped with modern facilities, from a sophisticated library to comfortable accommodation. It was a place designed to foster not just intellectual growth but spiritual depth as well. As I walked through the serene campus, I felt a sense of awe. The Lord had led me to a place where I could grow, both academically and spiritually. The verses of Isaiah 40:31 echoed in my heart, "But those who hope in the Lord will renew their strength. They will soar on wings like eagles; they will run and not grow weary, they will walk and not be faint."

The theological education offered at the seminary was top-notch. Our teachers, who were not just learned scholars but deeply godly individuals, imparted more than just knowledge. They taught us how to live out the gospel in every area of life. We studied the Scriptures in depth, learning the original languages of Hebrew and Greek, church history, missions, and practical theology. It was intense, but it was precisely what I needed to be equipped for the mission God had laid on my heart.

Grateful for the Leaders

I am especially grateful to Dr. K.P. Yohannan, the founder of Gospel for Asia, for his vision to create such an environment. He had built a seminary where students like me, who had no means to afford education, could receive the best theological training free of charge. It was a rare opportunity, and I knew that I must make the most of it. As Proverbs 16:3 reminds us, "Commit to the Lord whatever you do, and he will establish your plans."

Dr. Packiam T. Samuel, the registrar of the seminary, was like a father to all of us. His heart for the poor and needy students, especially for someone like me who came with very little, was truly Christlike. He arranged part-time work for many of us, ensuring that we had enough to meet our basic needs while studying. I will never forget the kindness he showed me, which strengthened my resolve to press on during difficult times. Through him and others, God provided a way for me to survive and thrive in the seminary.

A Time of Growth and Zeal

The three years I spent at GFA seminary were transformative. Not only was I equipped with a quality theological education, but I was also molded into a servant of Christ with a deeper passion for missions. I learned that God doesn't just call us to study His Word—He calls us to live it out and share it with others, especially those who have never heard of His love. This echoed the Great Commission in Matthew 28:19-20: "Therefore go and make disciples of all nations, baptizing them in the name of the Father and of the Son and of the Holy Spirit, and teaching them to obey everything I have commanded you. And surely, I am with you always, to the very end of the age."

Mission zeal was instilled in every student at the seminary. We were taught to carry the gospel to the ends of the earth, no matter the cost. My heart burned with passion to serve the Lord in remote places, to bring the good news to those who had never heard it. It was a fire that was ignited during my time in Hyderabad, and it only grew stronger during my studies in Kerala.

I also learned the importance of godly character. Theological education was not just about acquiring knowledge but about shaping our hearts to reflect Christ. Our teachers emphasized integrity, humility, and sacrificial love—traits that were essential for anyone called to serve in the mission field. I knew that the Lord was preparing me for something great, though I did not yet fully understand the scope of His plans.

The training period at Gospel for Asia (GFA) was one of the most formative times of my life, filled with moments of profound spiritual growth, dependence on the Lord, and the development of an unwavering trust in His provision. During this time, I learned that God is faithful to provide for every need, sometimes in ways that we cannot comprehend, and often in His perfect timing.

All-Night Prayers: Sweet Memories

One of the most memorable aspects of my time at GFA was the monthly all-night prayers. These nights of extended prayer were powerful, life-transforming moments where we felt the presence of the Holy Spirit moving among us. We would gather at 8 p.m. and continue in prayer until the early hours of the morning—sometimes until 4 a.m., and on rare occasions, even until 7 a.m.

These nights were filled with intercession, worship, and deep communion with God. As we sought the Lord together, I often found myself praying for hours without realizing the time passing. It was as if heaven had opened, and we were participating in divine fellowship. The words of Jesus in Matthew 18:20 rang true during these times: "For where two or three gather in my name, there am I with them."

Trusting God for My Needs

Despite the spiritual richness I experienced, my time at GFA was not without challenges, especially in the area of finances. I had no sponsorship or financial support from my parents. Yet, through these trials, the Lord was teaching me to trust Him for even the most basic needs.

There were months when I would go without money in my hand, but I never let my faith waver. Like the widow's oil in 2 Kings 4:1-7, God continued to provide, often at the last moment, but always just enough to meet my needs. My dependence on Him grew deeper as I learned that He is Jehovah Jireh, my Provider (Genesis 22:14).

One particular incident stands out in my memory. I had fallen severely ill and had no money to go to the hospital. My sickness lingered for two months, and I endured it, trusting that God would provide a way. One of our teachers, Mr. Judia Berdan, noticed my condition and, without hesitation, took me to the hospital and paid my medical bills. This act of kindness was a clear reminder of God's care through His people. As Philippians 4:19 says, "And my God will meet all your needs according to the riches of his glory in Christ Jesus." The Lord continued to meet my needs in ways that were beyond my understanding.

God's Provision Through Others

I was also blessed by the constant support from the Tenali Evangelical Union (EU) and Evangelical Graduate Fellowship (EGF) well-wishers. Their prayers sustained me through difficult times, and the JMJ College students' prayer cell in Tenali generously contributed to my needs. Mrs. Santha Kumari and Mrs. Manjula played a pivotal role in initiating this support, and I am forever grateful to them.

One of the most touching moments came when Mrs. Santha Kumari introduced me to Mrs. Rukmini, a devout believer in Christ, although she came from a Hindu background. She extended motherly love toward me, taking care of me as if I were her own son. She, along with her friend Mrs. Padma, collected funds and sent me contributions that helped me survive. Their godliness and generosity were manifestations of God's grace in my life.

These acts of kindness reminded me of the early church described in Acts 4:34-35, where "there were no needy persons among them," because the believers shared what they had. I felt that same spirit of love and unity during my time at GFA.

7. Praying for My Family's Salvation

While I was focusing on my M. Div. studies, another burden weighed heavily on my heart: the salvation of my family. My parents and sister were still followers of the Hindu faith, and for four years, I had been praying fervently for their salvation. Despite my constant prayers, letters, and even sending Bibles home, there was no visible change in their attitude toward the Gospel. But I held on to the promise of Acts 16:31, "Believe in the Lord Jesus, and you will be saved—you and your household."

In November 1998, during my second year of M.Div studies, something extraordinary happened. One evening, after a long day of studying in the seminary library, a heavy downpour of rain trapped me and my close friends. It was impossible to return to our rooms. One of my friends, Mr. Williams, suggested that we use this opportunity to pray. We knelt in front of the library and began to pray for our personal needs and burdens. I prayed earnestly for my family's salvation, crying out to God with everything in me. Mr. Williams encouraged me, saying, "Let us believe that your family will be saved in a few months, by faith." We continued praying until midnight, despite the rain still pouring down. The presence of God was so strong, and it felt as though fire from heaven had descended upon us. I believed, without any doubt, that God was going to answer my prayer.

7.1 The Miracle for My Family

Just a week later, I received a letter from my mother. In it, she shared that my sister, Malleswary, had been tormented by sleeplessness for months. They had gone to several temples and consulted many doctors, but nothing had worked. My mother, who had previously been resistant to the Gospel, made a desperate request: she asked me to come home and pray to my God, Jesus, for healing.

I could hardly believe what I was reading. This was the breakthrough I had been praying for! I shouted, "Hallelujah!" and jumped for joy as I realized that my family was now open to the power of Christ.

I went home during the Christmas holidays with great anticipation and joy. When I arrived, I prayed for my sister Malleswary, asking the Lord to bring her peace and healing. For the first time in six months, she slept peacefully that night. This visible demonstration of God's power deeply impacted both my mother and my sister. While my father remained hardened and even grew more hostile toward the Gospel, my mother and sister accepted the Lord with joy.

7.2 Discipling My Family

During the one-month holiday, I stayed home and took every opportunity to disciple my mother and sister. We would read the Bible together, pray, and talk about the transformative power of Jesus. It was an incredible time of spiritual growth for them, and I could see the Lord working in their hearts. As Jesus said in John 4:35, "Open your eyes and look at the fields! They are ripe for harvest."

Even though my father resisted and sometimes became angry, I held onto the belief that God would one day soften his heart as well. With my mother and sister now walking in the faith, I returned to college with renewed strength and a deeper conviction that nothing is impossible with God (Luke 1:37).

My journey at GFA was filled with moments of hardship, but every step was a testimony to God's faithfulness. He not only provided for my physical needs through generous believers, but He also answered my deepest prayers for my family's salvation. The Lord taught me that faith and persistence in prayer are powerful and that His timing is always perfect.

As I continued my studies, I knew that God had a great purpose for my life and ministry. My time at GFA was shaping me into the servant He was calling me to be—a servant willing to go wherever He would send me, trusting Him every step of the way. As Psalm 37:5 encourages us, "Commit your way to the Lord; trust in him and he will do this." The lessons I learned at GFA would stay with me for the rest of my life, reminding me that no matter how difficult the circumstances, God is always present, guiding, providing, and working out His perfect plan.

8. A Spiritual Battle and God's Deliverance

As I entered the final year of my studies at Gospel for Asia, I was full of hope and anticipation for the future. The Lord had been faithful throughout my journey, and I was earnestly seeking His guidance for the next steps in my life. However, I did not anticipate the intense spiritual warfare that would unfold during this crucial time. My health began to deteriorate rapidly, and without explanation, I found myself unable to sleep—often going without rest for days on end. For nearly six months, I battled insomnia, and it took a heavy toll on both my physical and mental well-being.

The strain of my final-year studies added to the pressure. As the academic workload increased, so did the weight on my shoulders. There were nights when I had no choice but to stay up all night completing assignments or preparing for presentations, even though I had barely slept for days. The exhaustion was overwhelming, and at one point, I seriously considered quitting the program. I remember crying out to God, asking, "Lord, how can I continue like this?" But deep within, I knew that there was nowhere else for me to go and that giving up was not an option. The words of Psalm 55:22 sustained me: "Cast your cares on the LORD and he will sustain you; he will never let the righteous be shaken."

Despite my determination to press on, the spiritual attack intensified. One evening, as I stood on the terrace of the hostel's fifth floor, overwhelmed with despair and exhaustion, I heard a dark voice whisper to me: "Jump. End it now. No one understands your pain. No one will care if you are gone." The enemy was trying to convince me that my life was worthless, that death was the only way out of my suffering.

For a moment, the temptation felt overpowering. But I clung to the promises of God, remembering James 4:7: "Submit yourselves, then, to God. Resist the devil, and he will flee from you." I cried out to the Lord with all my strength, refusing to give in to the enemy's lies. I knew that my life belonged to God and that He had a purpose for me. The Holy Spirit empowered me to resist, and I walked away from that dangerous edge.

Recognizing the seriousness of the spiritual battle I was facing, I decided to fast and seek the Lord earnestly for deliverance. I dedicated several days to fasting and prayer, asking God to intervene in my situation and to break the chains that were binding me. By January, after months of struggle, the Lord brought me the deliverance I so desperately needed. The sleepless nights came to an end, and I was filled with a renewed sense of peace. His Word was my refuge during this time, especially the promise of Psalm 34:4: "I sought the LORD, and he answered me; he delivered me from all my fears."

With three months left before graduation, I could finally focus on completing my studies. However, the battle had taught me an invaluable lesson: that spiritual warfare is real, but so is the power of God to overcome it. Through it all, the Lord never left my side, and He strengthened me in ways I could not have imagined.

9. Discipleship in Action:Impacting Lives with UESI

Seeking God's Direction for the Next Step

As I neared the end of my studies, my thoughts naturally turned to the future. I sought the Lord in prayer, asking Him to reveal the next step in my journey. There were several opportunities available to me, including prestigious ministry positions within Gospel for Asia itself. Many of these positions were high-profile and would have given me visibility and influence within the Christian community. However, despite these appealing offers, I had no peace about accepting them.

I spent weeks praying, asking God for clarity, but the answer was always the same—"Not this." At times, I wondered if I was missing God's direction, but I remained obedient to His leading, trusting that He would reveal His perfect will in due time. Proverbs 3:5-

6 became my guide during this season: "Trust in the LORD with all your heart and lean not on your own understanding; in all your ways submit to him, and he will make your paths straight."

One morning, as I was praying and continuing to seek God's guidance, I received the *Vidyarthi Jwala* monthly magazine from UESI-AP. Even though I had been away from student ministry due to my studies, my heart was still deeply connected to that mission. As I flipped through the pages of the magazine, an article caught my eye. It was a call to action—challenging believers to consider full-time ministry to disciple students in Andhra Pradesh.

As I read those words, it was as if the Lord Himself was speaking directly to me. The Holy Spirit stirred within me, and I knew at that moment that God was calling me back to student ministry. The clarity I had been praying for had finally arrived. There was no doubt in my mind that this was my next step. The Lord wanted me to return to Andhra Pradesh and join the movement to disciple and mentor the next generation of students. Matthew 28:19-20 echoed in my heart: "Therefore go and make disciples of all nations, baptizing them in the name of the Father and of the Son and of the Holy Spirit, and teaching them to obey everything I have commanded you."

9.1 The Mission Begins

The decision to return to Andhra Pradesh and join UESI was not just a career choice—it was a calling. I realized that God had been preparing me for this moment all along. Every trial, every challenge, and every victory during my time at Gospel for Asia had been equipping me for the mission that lay ahead. My heart was filled with excitement and anticipation as I thought about the lives that could be transformed through the power of the gospel.

I understood that the journey ahead would not be easy. The challenges of ministry are many, and the enemy would certainly try to hinder the work. But I also knew that God's hand was upon me and that His purposes could not be thwarted. Philippians 1:6 encouraged me: "Being confident of this, that he who began a good work in you will carry it on to completion until the day of Christ Jesus."

And so, with graduation behind me and a clear sense of God's direction before me, I embarked on the next chapter of my journey—dedicated to discipling students, sharing the love of Christ, and walking in the calling that God had placed on my life. The rest, as they say, is history.

As I reflect on the path that led me to join UESI (Union of Evangelical Students of India) as a full-time staff member, it becomes clear to me that this was a journey predestined by God. Though the road to discipleship was filled with challenges, temptations, and difficult decisions, the hand of God unmistakably guided every step, directing me toward His will.

After my M. Div. graduation in March 2000, I found myself at a critical crossroads. Many opportunities came my way, including potential positions in prestigious organizations, yet the Lord continually closed those doors, steering me in a specific direction. I had previously applied to RZIM (Ravi Zacharias International Ministries) and didn't initially think they would consider my application. I attended their national seminars, where I had been trained by Mr. L.T. Jeyachandran, the Executive Director of RZIM's Asia-Pacific branch. He was a brilliant mind, deeply rooted in the Word, and had been instrumental in shaping my Spiritual and Theological perspectives.

Moreover, Mr. Sudhakar Mondithoka, who played a fatherly role in my spiritual journey, was already working with RZIM in a significant position and had recommended me for a role in the ministry. The thought of joining such an esteemed organization filled me with excitement, and it seemed that they were quite positive about bringing me on board. Little did I know that this would turn out to be another lesson in listening to God's whisper over earthly appeal.

A Letter Lost to Time

In January 2000, as I prepared for my final exams, I had no idea that a letter from RZIM was making its way to my parents' house in Guntur. I didn't have a permanent address of my own at the time—I was a wanderer, moving from place to place, wherever the Lord led me. My father, however, was not a believer and had no understanding of the importance of that letter. He threw it into the garbage without informing me. When I visited my family in May 2000, I was completely unaware that my chance to join RZIM had been discarded with that letter.

However, as Romans 8:28 reminds us, "And we know that in all things God works for the good of those who love him, who have been called according to his purpose." This incident, though initially disheartening, was not a loss but part of God's perfect plan.

A Warm Welcome to UESI

During that same month of May 2000, I had an interview with UESI-AP (Andhra Pradesh) leaders. From the moment I walked into their office, I felt a sense of belonging. The warm welcome from the UESI family was like an embrace from God Himself, confirming that I was where He wanted me to be. Once they confirmed my acceptance as a staff member, without hesitation, I signed the papers to join UESI as a full-time field staff member, effective from June 1, 2000. This step felt like a divine alignment with the calling I had sensed for years—the Lord was leading me into a ministry of discipleship, evangelism, and mentoring students in the Gospel.

A Temptation at Khandala, Mumbai

Soon after joining UESI, I had a pre-planned commitment to attend RZIM's 3rd phase national seminar at Khandala, Mumbai, in the last week of June

2000. I took leave from my new role and made my way to the conference, eager to learn and connect with my mentors. As I entered the meeting room on the first day, I was greeted warmly by Mr. L.T. Jeyachandran.

"Venkat, we sent you an interview letter. Why didn't you respond?" he asked, his voice full of curiosity and expectation. Before I could explain, he added, "That's okay. We are looking for a coordinator to initiate the ministry in Mumbai, and we were thinking of you for this role. We can have the interview now and finish the deal."

His words hit me like a wave. Here was an opportunity to work with RZIM, an organization I deeply respected. They were offering me a role that many would consider prestigious, with a good salary and the chance to make a significant impact. The temptation was real, and for a brief moment, I was tempted to say yes.

But as Proverbs 16:9 reminds us, "In their hearts humans plan their course, but the Lord establishes their steps." In that moment of decision, I felt the Lord whisper into my heart, reminding me of the commitment I had made just two weeks earlier with

UESI. I had already signed the papers. My word mattered, and I knew that integrity and faithfulness to the path God had set before me were more important than worldly prestige or financial security.

I explained to Mr. L.T. that I had never seen their interview letter and that I had already joined UESI. It was a humble decision and a difficult one, but I knew it was the right choice. The path of discipleship often involves carrying our cross, and this was one such moment for me. I chose to stay faithful to UESI, trusting that God had led me there for a purpose, even though the salary was minimal and the responsibilities were many.

9.2 Taking Up the Cross

Choosing UESI over RZIM was not just a career decision—it was a spiritual one. At that time, my family was going through significant changes. My mother and sister had recently come to faith in Christ and were growing as new believers. My father, however, remained indifferent to our needs and offered little support. My mother had suffered much, and I had a deep desire to earn good money to help them and improve their situation. The thought of a well-paying job with RZIM was tempting, but I knew I needed to take up my cross and follow the Lord's call, even if it meant financial sacrifice.

As Jesus says in Matthew 16:24, "Whoever wants to be my disciple must deny themselves and take up their cross and follow me." This was my cross—choosing a ministry that didn't promise financial stability but offered the opportunity to impact lives for Christ.

Despite the challenges, I found joy in serving Him. It was humbling, but I knew that this was where God had called me to be. My decision to stay with UESI was a defining moment in my spiritual journey, one that solidified my commitment to discipleship and the mission of spreading the Gospel.

UESI: A Ministry of Transformation

My time with UESI has been a season of transformation, both in my own life and in the lives of the students I have had the privilege to disciple. Through Bible studies, prayer meetings, and one-on-one mentoring, I have seen God move in powerful ways. Students who once lived without purpose found their calling in Christ, and many went on to serve in ministry themselves.

Discipleship is not merely about teaching—it's about living out the Gospel in action. As James 1:22 says, "Do not merely listen to the word, and so deceive yourselves. Do what it says." At UESI, I learned that true discipleship is about embodying Christ's love and sacrifice in everything we do.

I have seen God provide for me and my family in miraculous ways, even when our financial resources were scarce. He has been faithful, sustaining me through seasons of difficulty and blessing me with opportunities to serve His people.

9.3 A Humble Beginning with a Greater Purpose

Joining UESI was not just a job—it was the beginning of a lifelong calling. As I look back on that decision in June 2000, I see God's hand guiding me through every step. Though it was a humble beginning, it set the stage for a ministry that would impact countless lives for Christ.

In the next section of this chapter, I will share more about my ministry experiences with UESI, the challenges we faced, and the victories we saw by God's grace. Through it all, I have learned that true discipleship is about surrendering to God's will, even when the path is difficult, and trusting that He will lead us into His perfect plan. "For I know the plans I have for you," declares the Lord, "plans to prosper you and not to harm you, plans to give you hope and a future." (Jeremiah 29:11).

9.4 Ministry in Paloncha
Paloncha: A Quiet Town with Deep Spiritual Roots

Paloncha, a small industrial town nestled in the lush landscapes of East Telangana, has always been known for its serene environment and simplicity. The town, primarily dominated by the workforce of the Kothagudem Thermal Power Station and Singareni Collieries, stands as a silent witness to the hustle and bustle of industrial life. Paloncha's streets are lined with simple houses, and its people lead humble, hardworking lives. The heat of the sun and the dust rising from the unpaved roads paint a picture of perseverance. However, beneath this ordinary façade, Paloncha was about to become a place of extraordinary spiritual significance, not just for me but for all those I encountered.

I arrived in Paloncha at the age of 24, young

and full of zeal, yet somewhat overwhelmed by the weight of the responsibility that lay ahead of me. I had been assigned the enormous task of overseeing the Evangelical Union (EU) and Evangelical Graduate Fellowship (EGF) ministries across five vast districts—Khammam, Karimnagar, Warangal, Nizamabad, and Adilabad. These districts encompassed large urban areas, countless small towns, and remote villages, each with its own culture, challenges, and spiritual needs.

I can still recall the sense of awe and trembling anticipation as I stepped into this new chapter of my life. At such a young age, I felt like a small, insignificant vessel chosen for a monumental task. The words of the Apostle Paul in 2 Corinthians 12:9 came to mind often: "But he said to me, 'My grace is sufficient for you, for my power is made perfect in weakness.' Therefore, I will boast all the more gladly of my weaknesses, so that the power of Christ may rest upon me." It was in my perceived weaknesses that I knew God's strength would be revealed.

The Concept of Hands-On Discipleship

Before going further into the details of my

ministry in Paloncha, I must explain the concept of **Hands-On Discipleship**—a phrase that became pivotal in shaping my approach to leadership and ministry during this season of my life. Hands-on discipleship, to me, signifies a personal, active, and deeply involved style of spiritual mentorship. It is not merely about teaching or imparting knowledge from a distance, but about walking with people in their spiritual journey, equipping them through real-life experiences, struggles, and victories.

I learned that true discipleship was about more than leading Bible studies or giving sermons. It involved living out the gospel daily in front of those whom God had entrusted to me. It required showing them how to pray by praying with them, teaching them how to serve by serving alongside them, and demonstrating the love of God through my own actions and care for their lives. It was in this **hands-on** approach—living with the people, sharing meals, traveling together, and engaging in the daily realities of life—that deep spiritual formation occurred.

This philosophy of discipleship was shaped by the example of Christ Himself, who, during His earthly ministry, lived among His disciples, teaching them through His words and actions, and giving them opportunities to minister alongside Him. My time in Paloncha required me to follow that model closely, involving myself deeply in the lives of those I was leading and mentoring.

The Welcoming in Paloncha

My entry into Paloncha was marked by a humble yet memorable welcome. The first meeting was arranged at the home of Mr. Suvarna Rao, a local EGF member. His modest house became the base for what would be a deeply fulfilling year of **hands-on discipleship** and ministry. As I stood before the gathering of local believers that evening, there was a noticeable air of hesitation. Later, Sister Mary, a faithful EGF member in the ministry, would tell me her initial thoughts: "What can this small, tiny, weak boy do? How can he manage this ministry?" It was a sentiment I didn't take offense to, for in many ways, I had felt the same. But I was reminded of the story of David, a young shepherd boy whom God chose to defeat the giant, Goliath, through divine empowerment. I clung to this promise, trusting that just as God had empowered David, He would equip me for the work ahead.

Despite the initial skepticism, God was gracious to me. Over the next few months, the local EU and EGF members in Paloncha and across the five districts opened their hearts and homes to me. I found a sense of spiritual family that I had never known before. The early church described in Acts 2:42-47 became my living reality, as believers shared everything in common, ministered together, and sought God with one heart. I am ever grateful to Mr. Ramakrishna, a man of great faith and generosity, who not only provided my accommodation in Paloncha but also became like a brother to me. His house was my resting place, a refuge in times of physical and emotional weariness.

9.4.1 My Prayer Time on the Mountain

Amidst the bustling responsibilities of ministry, I carved out a special time for prayer and solitude atop a nearby mountain. This mountain became my sacred sanctuary, a place where I could escape the demands of daily life and draw closer to God. Whenever I was in the town, I would rise before dawn, climb to the summit, and find a quiet spot to sit in His presence.

It was here, surrounded by nature's beauty and serenity, that I poured out my heart to God. I sought His wisdom and guidance for the ministry, interceded for the students and families I was working with, and asked for strength to fulfill the responsibilities placed upon me. The tranquility of the mountain provided an atmosphere conducive to deep reflection and spiritual connection. As I gazed out over the valleys below, I was reminded of God's vastness and His unchanging nature. I would often pray the words of Psalm 121:1-2, "I lift up my eyes to the mountains—where does my help come from? My help comes from the LORD, the Maker of heaven and earth."

These prayer times became transformative moments in my life. I experienced clarity in decision-making and a deeper assurance of God's presence in my ministry. It was during one of these sessions that I felt the Lord impress upon my heart the importance of sharing my journey with others, encouraging them to seek their own intimate relationship with Him.

9.4.2 Ministry in Motion: Traveling and Teaching
The responsibility I carried meant that I

couldn't stay in one place for long. I had been given charge over a region that covered hundreds of miles, with numerous colleges and university campuses scattered across the five districts. My schedule was packed with travel, and it wasn't unusual for me to be on the road for 25 days out of every month. My mission was clear: to teach, train, and mentor the EU and EGF groups that were already in place, as well as to establish new ministries in colleges that had yet to be reached.

As part of my probationary training, I was required to read numerous theological books, prepare doctrines, and engage deeply with foundational texts that would equip me for effective ministry. This training included visiting key leaders in various cities and attending rigorous training sessions in Kotagiri, Tamil Nadu. The mountainous backdrop of Kotagiri provided a refreshing contrast to my ministry in the plains, fostering an environment where I could absorb the teachings and interact with seasoned leaders.

In these training sessions, I learned about leadership, evangelism, and church growth. I studied the writings of early church fathers, the importance of sound doctrine, and effective methods of outreach.

This foundation prepared me to engage more thoughtfully with the students I would encounter in Paloncha, helping me to answer their questions with clarity and confidence.

It was through this extensive travel and personal interaction that I implemented **hands-on discipleship** most effectively. Whether in a classroom setting, during a student retreat, or even over a simple meal, I sought to disciple the students and graduates through every aspect of life. We prayed together, shared our burdens, and faced challenges as one body. Every interaction became a teaching moment, not only for those I led but also for me as I learned the value of relational ministry.

Traveling in those days was not easy. The roads were rough, and public transportation was unreliable. Many times, I would be dropped off at the outskirts of a village or town, and I would have to walk several miles to reach my destination. Yet, each step I took was filled with purpose. It reminded me of the journeys of the early apostles, who traveled far and wide to spread the gospel despite the hardships they faced. As the Apostle Paul wrote in Romans 10:15, "How beautiful are the feet of those who bring good news!" I believed that every step I took in faith would bring the good news of Christ to those in need.

9.4.3 Family Restoration

One of the most significant aspects of my time in Paloncha was the way in which **hands-on discipleship** played a crucial role in healing and restoring my relationship with my family. Paloncha was located near my parents' place, and unbeknownst to me, God had already been working in their hearts long before I arrived. My grandfather, Sri. Lakshminarayana had established an ashram on 25 acres of land near Paloncha. After his passing, my parents inherited this land and moved to the area to settle. By the time I arrived, my parents and sister had already relocated, and my brother had established himself in Guntur.

It was a beautiful and divine coincidence that as I began my ministry in Paloncha, I also had the opportunity to reconnect with my family. I frequently visited them, and over time, I witnessed God's transformative power in their lives. Through prayer, patience, and the model of **hands-on discipleship**, my family began to see the fruit of a faith-filled life. We spent quality time together, sharing meals, praying, and engaging in conversations about the Lord.

During one of my visits, I could see a shift in my parents' attitudes toward faith and ministry. My mother, who had experienced much pain due to my father's earlier abandonment, began to express hope and renewal. It was evident that God was working in their hearts, restoring broken relationships and healing past wounds.

This season of ministry not only shaped the lives of the students and young adults I worked with but also marked the beginning of healing and restoration in my family. As I embraced **hands-on discipleship**, I learned that it wasn't just about leading others to Christ; it was also about being open to the healing work of God in my own life and relationships. God's grace was at work in every facet of my ministry, and I was in awe of how He orchestrated it all.

9.4.4 A Year of Harvest

The year I spent in Paloncha was undoubtedly one of the most fruitful and spiritually rewarding times of my life. Despite my initial uncertainties, God used me to build His kingdom in ways I never thought possible. Through **hands-on discipleship**, I witnessed countless students, graduates, and families grow in their faith, step into their callings, and experience personal transformation.

By the end of the year, the EU and EGF ministries across the five districts were flourishing, with new groups being formed in previously unreached colleges. It was a year of abundant spiritual harvest.

As I look back on that year, I am filled with gratitude for the way God used me in my weakness to accomplish His purposes. Paloncha became a place of personal growth, family restoration, and fruitful ministry, all made possible by God's grace and His unfailing faithfulness. **Hands-on discipleship** was the cornerstone of that ministry, enabling me to deeply invest in the lives of those God had entrusted to me—not through words alone, but through actions, shared struggles, and victories in Christ.

9.5 Ministry and Mentorship in Warangal

My time in Warangal from 2001 to 2003 was a pivotal period in my spiritual journey and ministry. Transitioning from the smaller town of Paloncha to this vibrant city marked a significant shift in my responsibilities and opportunities for growth. Warangal, with its rich cultural heritage and academic institutions, became a fertile ground for ministry and discipleship. During these three years, I engaged deeply with students and established meaningful relationships that fostered both personal and communal growth in faith. This section encapsulates the essence of my experiences in Warangal, highlighting the powerful impact of hands-on discipleship, mentorship, and the invaluable friendships formed during this transformative season.

Warangal: A City Rich in History and Spirit

Warangal, a city steeped in history and spiritual significance, is located in the heart of Telangana, India. It is known for its rich cultural heritage, evident in its ancient temples, forts, and the picturesque landscapes surrounding it. Once the capital of the Kakatiya dynasty, Warangal boasts majestic structures like the Warangal Fort and the Thousand Pillar Temple, which narrate tales of valor and devotion. The city is a blend of modernity and tradition, where bustling markets coexist with serene temples, and the vibrant life of its residents reflects a unique tapestry of faith and culture.

Warangal is not just a geographical location; it is a hub of education and spirituality. The city is home to several prestigious educational institutions, including the National Institute of Technology (NIT), which attracts students from all over the country. This blend of academic rigor and cultural richness provides a fertile ground for ministry and discipleship. The people of Warangal are known for their warmth and hospitality, creating an environment where relationships can flourish. It is this welcoming atmosphere that set the stage for my next chapter of ministry and mentorship.

As I arrived in Warangal, I felt a profound sense of purpose and excitement. The transition from Paloncha to Warangal marked not just a geographical shift but a significant elevation in my responsibilities and opportunities for spiritual growth.

9.5.1 A New Chapter Begins

After successfully completing my probationary period, I received a formal confirmation from our state secretary, Mr. Edward W. Kuntam. His letter stated that I should shift my base from Paloncha to Warangal, a bigger town with greater potential for ministry. I was filled with anticipation as I read those words. It was a chance to expand my reach and influence in the lives of students and young adults.

On June 1, 2001, I reported to Professor Anand Raj at NIT, Warangal. As I entered the campus, the vibrant atmosphere, filled with students bustling between classes and activities, invigorated my spirit. I was welcomed with open arms by Professor Anand Raj and other EGF members of the city—Mr. Yadagiri, Mr. Amardev Prasad, Mr. L. Samuel, Mr. David, and several others. Their respect for my role and eagerness to collaborate was humbling, especially given their distinguished backgrounds and experience.

The words of Proverbs 27:17 came to mind: "As iron sharpens iron, so one person sharpens another." I knew that working alongside these respected graduates would not only enhance my ministry but also foster my personal growth. The support and wisdom they offered created a nurturing environment for me to flourish, despite my youth.

9.5.2 Respect and Acceptance Amidst Youth

Though I was considerably younger than most

of the individuals I worked with, I was met with respect and acceptance. They listened intently as I shared the Word of God, creating an atmosphere conducive to learning and spiritual growth. It was a unique privilege to teach and mentor students in a setting where tradition and modernity intertwined, and I found myself blessed to lead a group of mature and committed believers.

Warangal was ideally situated as a central point for my ministry, well connected by trains and buses to various colleges and Kakatiya University in the region. This accessibility allowed me to travel extensively and engage with a diverse range of students. The opportunities for outreach were plentiful, and I quickly began to establish a network of Evangelical Union (EU) students eager to learn and grow in their faith.

9.5.3 A Flourishing Ministry of Discipleship

My time in Warangal became a fruitful season of **hands-on discipleship**. The students in this town were not only eager to learn; they were also passionate about living out their faith. We engaged in deep discussions, shared meals, and prayed together. The friendships formed during this period were characterized by authenticity and a shared commitment to following Christ.

The students' enthusiasm for ministry was infectious, and I found joy in leading college and university students throughout the region. As I taught the Word of God, I emphasized the importance of applying biblical principles in everyday life. James 1:22 reminds us, "Do not merely listen to the word, and so deceive yourselves. Do what it says." This became a foundational verse for our gatherings, challenging each of us to live out our faith actively.

The EU students in Warangal had remarkable maturity for their age. They understood the challenges faced by young believers in a secular world and were committed to supporting one another in their spiritual journeys. Together, we organized events, outreach programs, and study groups that not only strengthened our fellowship but also made an impact on the wider community.

The Gift of Fellowship

The fellowship I experienced during this time was a source of immense encouragement. We gathered regularly for prayer meetings, Bible studies, and outreach initiatives. Each event was marked by a sense of unity and purpose, as we sought to uplift one another in our spiritual walks.

I fondly remember one particular evening when we hosted a community gathering. Students from various backgrounds came together to share their testimonies and experiences of faith. The atmosphere was electric, filled with laughter, tears, and heartfelt worship. It was moments like these that reminded me of the beauty of the body of Christ, where every member plays a vital role in building one another up (Ephesians 4:16).

As I walked through the campuses, I often reflected on the profound impact that **hands-on discipleship** had on the lives of the students. I witnessed their growth in confidence, leadership skills, and a deeper understanding of Scripture. It was a blessing to be part of their journey and to see them step into their God-given callings and take bold steps in their faith.

10. A Significant Milestone: My Wedding

As my ministry flourished in Warangal, a significant milestone was on the horizon—my wedding. This chapter of my life would not only unite me with my beloved but also intertwine our ministry efforts. The journey of preparing for marriage added another layer of joy and excitement to my time in Warangal.

In the coming section, I will share the beautiful story of how I met my wife and the profound impact our union had on our ministry. Our shared vision and passion for serving God would be instrumental as we navigated the challenges and triumphs of married life while continuing our commitment to discipleship and mentorship in the region.

My transition to Warangal marked the beginning of an incredible season of ministry, learning, and fellowship. The **hands-on discipleship** approach I embraced not only enriched the lives of those I mentored but also deepened my understanding of God's calling in my life. As I embarked on this journey, I was reminded of the words in Isaiah 40:31: "But those who hope in the LORD will renew their strength. They will soar on wings like eagles; they will run and not grow weary, they will walk and not be faint." With hope in the Lord, I continued to move forward, eager to embrace the next chapter of my spiritual awakening in the vibrant city of Warangal.

10.1 A Sacred Bond

After years of witnessing the struggles my mother endured in her marriage, I developed a deep and sacred desire to build a family rooted in love, understanding, and faith. My mother's life was marked by intense suffering, much of which stemmed from societal pressures surrounding dowry, caste, and family pride. The prideful attitudes toward religious divisions, along with the inherent biases within the family system, created a backdrop of constant tension and unease in her life. The pain and hardship she went through left a profound mark on my heart, making me prayerfully consider what a God-centered marriage should look like from my early days of conversion.

From those tender moments when I first gave my life to Christ in 1993, I began praying earnestly for my future family. I didn't want a marriage that was simply an arrangement of societal convenience or familial expectation. Rather, I prayed for a partner who would walk with me in my spiritual journey and share in the ministry that the Lord had called me to. It was my firm belief that God would grant me the wisdom and grace to create a family that reflected His glory and love—something different from the traditions and customs that often bound others.

The godly families I encountered in our UESI (Union of Evangelical Students of India) ministry profoundly shaped my understanding of marriage and family. Many of these homes became beacons of spiritual light for me. They showed me the potential for a family built on a solid foundation of faith, where love and mutual respect could overcome the harsh realities of cultural norms. Observing their lives ignited a deep desire in my heart to have a marriage that was not only spiritually strong but also one that honored God in every aspect. I longed to create such a home for myself and my future partner—one where the love of Christ would reign supreme, and where faith would guide our decisions and interactions.

As I grew in my walk with the Lord, I also became more cautious about choosing a life partner. Coming from a traditional Hindu family, the challenge of making such a decision was immense. Caste, dowry, employment, and family status were deeply entrenched values within the culture I was raised in. The significance of these social structures could not be ignored, and I knew that I would need to navigate them carefully. There was also a significant cultural expectation regarding arranged marriages, where families, rather than individuals, had the final say in selecting a spouse. This dynamic often placed additional pressure on young people, who were expected to conform to their family's wishes, regardless of their personal convictions or spiritual desires.

For readers unfamiliar with the concept, **arranged marriage** is a practice deeply rooted in Indian culture. It is traditionally seen as a partnership between two families, not just between two individuals. In many cases, the decision is made based on compatibility between families, often prioritizing factors such as caste, financial status, and family reputation. The concept of **love marriage**—where two individuals fall in love and choose to marry without family intervention—was not only rare but also stigmatized, especially in rural South India. In fact, love marriages were viewed with skepticism and often met with severe criticism, as they were seen as rebellious and dishonoring to the family.

In this context, I faced a dilemma. From the moment I accepted Christ, relatives would mock me, making hurtful comments about my spiritual convictions and predicting that I would one day marry a girl from a lower caste, as a form of punishment or shame. Yet, by the grace of God, I remained calm and polite in the face of these insults, trusting that He had a better plan for my life. I believed that God's hand was upon my life, and I knew that He would provide a partner according to His perfect will.

During this period, one of my cousins, a close relative, began expressing a desire to give her daughter to me in marriage. This proposal came not from a place of love but from the societal expectations surrounding my growing status. I had just begun earning, established myself in ministry, and gained a degree of respect in my community. My cousin saw this as an opportunity to elevate her daughter's future. When I said no to her request, she was very angry and put a lot of pressure on me through other relatives, but I never yielded to such pressure.

I was always careful not to encourage such advances, as my heart was set on the Lord's timing and direction for my future partner. I knew that marrying someone based on familial pressure or societal expectations would not align with God's plan for my life.

In 2001, a significant turning point arrived. As I was actively engaged in ministry in Warangal, proposals started coming my way from various directions. My mentors began suggesting potential matches, while family members also exerted their influence. The pressure to marry was mounting from all sides—both within and outside of me. At times, I found myself wrestling with these expectations, unsure of how to proceed.

Amid this inner turmoil, I had a preplanned UESI study center training session in October 2001 at Kotagiri, located in the picturesque hills of Tamil Nadu. This was a month-long training program, and as I prepared for the journey, I felt a strange but strong sense that God would speak to me during this time away. I could feel the Lord guiding me, urging me to take this time to reflect and seek His will more earnestly. I remember vividly standing in the home of Mr. Edward Williams, the Andhra Pradesh state secretary of UESI, with my bags packed and ready to leave. It was during this moment that I overheard an interesting conversation. Mr. Vilbert, the Karnataka state secretary, was visiting, and as they talked, Vilbert made a passing comment that struck me deeply: "Williams, we have so many girls coming to Kotagiri for training. It's better you help a boy from Andhra get married to one of them."

Something about those words resonated within me. Even though they were said in a light-hearted manner, I felt as though God was whispering something deeper into my soul. Could it be that I would find my life partner at this training? Despite this stirring in my heart, I dared not speak of it. In our culture, we were careful not to engage with the opposite sex, especially in matters of love or marriage. It was considered highly inappropriate, and the idea of love marriages was looked down upon, often regarded as a sign of rebelliousness against family honor.

So, with my focus set firmly on the training, I left for Kotagiri. By then, I was well-trained theologically, having completed an M.Div and sharp in my academics. The training at Kotagiri turned out to be an incredibly spirit-filled, empowering, and relaxing experience. It was a much-needed retreat from the rigorous demands of ministry, allowing me to connect more deeply with God. Throughout this time, many of the UESI leaders shared stories of how they had met their spouses at similar training events, but I never imagined that I, too, would experience something similar.

During this training, I met a young woman named Rita, who had come from Karnataka. She was also attending the same training, but our interactions were purely formal and respectful. One day, something quite humorous happened. Being an active participant in all the activities, I was often at the forefront of discussions and tasks. Rita, like any other friend, approached me during one of these moments and, in a rather flustered state, said, "I married you." Her words took me by surprise, and they caused everyone around us to burst into laughter. What she meant to ask was if

I could lend her a book titled *I Married You* for a book review. In her nervousness, she had mixed up her words, but her slip of the tongue became something of a prophecy. Little did I know that her words would indeed come to pass in the near future.

At that time, neither of us had any intentions of marriage. We were both focused on our training and ministry work. However, I had developed a habit of writing letters to friends, a practice that I had maintained since my early days of ministry. After the training ended, I sent a casual postcard letter to all the participants, including Rita. For many in India, especially in traditional families, receiving personal mail was quite rare, especially for young women. There was often a sense of guardedness around communication, and privacy was not highly valued— anyone could read the contents of a postcard. But for Rita, that postcard was special. It was the first personal letter she had ever received in her life.

Unbeknownst to me, this simple gesture stirred something in her heart. Rita had been praying about her future and felt that I might be the person God had chosen for her. However, I had no such intentions or inclinations at that point.

About a year later, in 2002, we crossed paths again at a mission conference in Bangalore. During this time, Rita became more convinced that I was the right person for her. Still, I remained unaware of her feelings. I was focused on my ministry and seeking God's will for my life. There were other marriage proposals presented to me during this period, particularly two from Telangana, but the Lord did not give me peace about pursuing them.

In the summer of 2002, we attended a nationwide UESI staff meeting at UBS (Union Biblical Seminary) in Pune. This was a significant event where staff members from across India gathered for fellowship and training. Rita and I were both present, but again, I was deeply engrossed in the program and didn't interact with her much. On the final day of the meeting, as I was preparing to leave with my bag in hand, Rita approached me and handed me a letter. She asked me to read it immediately, but I didn't. Instead, I tucked it into my bag, deciding to read it after reaching the next destination. But in curiosity, I opened the letter after reaching the room.

I had no idea how swiftly life could change until I found myself holding Rita's letter, standing at a crossroads of my own fate. It was a warm summer afternoon in 2002 at the UESI nationwide staff meeting held at the Union Biblical Seminary (UBS) in Pune. The air was filled with the excitement of the conference, yet at that moment, my mind was flooded with confusion, fear, and a strange sense of anticipation.

When Rita handed me the letter, her eyes were intense but calm, as though she had already made peace with what she was about to say. She asked me to read it before I left the campus. This was no ordinary request. My heart raced as I opened it, barely able to contain my thoughts. The letter was clear, direct, and unambiguous. She believed that God had spoken to her, leading her to believe that we were meant to marry. She explained that this decision needed to be finalized before I left the campus gate.

The weight of her words hit me like a storm. It was terrifying. How could I respond to such a profound statement? If I agreed, there was the fear that people would suspect that we had been secretly in love all along. That could lead to dangerous misunderstandings. UESI had strict codes of conduct, and rumors could easily cost me my job. The organization was my life, my ministry, and my future. Yet, the very idea of marriage filled me with hope and excitement. For years, I had prayed for a godly partner who would support my ministry and spiritual growth. But this? This was far more sudden and direct than I had imagined.

I felt overwhelmed by conflicting emotions. Should I take this as a divine intervention or a trap that could ruin my reputation? The tension between culture and divine calling weighed heavily on me. The South Indian culture I grew up in had strong boundaries around love, marriage, and relationships between men and women. Arranged marriages were the norm, and love marriages were often met with disdain and suspicion. A "love marriage" could bring accusations of impropriety, especially within the conservative Christian circles I belonged to.

In that moment of chaos, God gave me wisdom. The verse from Proverbs came to mind: *"Trust in the Lord with all your heart and lean not on your own understanding; in all your ways submit to Him, and He will make your paths straight"* (Proverbs 3:5-6, NIV). I knew I needed to surrender my confusion and fear to God. I have learned over the years to trust His leading, especially in moments of uncertainty. But how was I to proceed?

Without hesitating, I went directly to my boss, Mr. Edward, who was the UESI state secretary of Andhra Pradesh. I handed him the letter, explaining everything honestly and transparently. "Please read this, and do what the Lord leads you to do," I said, feeling the weight of my fear lift slightly as I surrendered the situation to someone wiser and more experienced.

Mr. Edward read the letter calmly, took a moment, and then looked at me. He assured me that there was nothing wrong with the situation and that we would handle it properly, involving the right people in the decision-making process. By bringing the matter into the open, I felt a strange sense of peace. The enemy thrives in secrecy, but when we bring things into the light, God can work mightily.

10.2 How I Found God's Will in My

Marriage

The journey towards finding God's will in my marriage was a profound experience, marked by prayer, fasting, and divine confirmation. After I handed over Rita's letter to Mr. Williams and returned to Paloncha, I felt an overwhelming need to seek God's guidance. The weight of this decision loomed over me, and I wanted to be sure that I was not merely being swayed by external circumstances but was genuinely following God's plan for my life.

10.2.1 The Decision to Fast

Determined to listen to God's voice and discern His will, I embarked on a five-day fast. This was not just any fast; I decided to abstain from all food, consuming only water. Fasting has always been a spiritual discipline that deepens my reliance on God, allowing me to focus on prayer and His Word. As I set aside my physical needs, my heart and mind were drawn closer to the Lord. This fast was a sacred time, where I sought to clear away the noise of life and find clarity in God's purpose.

The first day of fasting was challenging. My body protested against the absence of food, but my spirit craved the nourishment that only comes from communion with God. Each passing hour felt like a spiritual exercise, honing my focus on the Lord. I spent time in prayer, earnestly seeking God's direction for my future with Rita. I knew this was a significant decision that would shape the rest of my life, and I wanted to honor God in every aspect of it.

10.2.2 Seeking God's Voice

During this intense time of seeking, I immersed myself in Scripture, hoping to hear God's voice through His Word. As I read, one particular verse stood out to me: *"Trust in the LORD with all your heart and lean not on your own understanding; in all your ways acknowledge him, and he will make your paths straight"* (Proverbs 3:5-6). This verse resonated deeply within me, confirming that my trust in God was paramount in this decision-making process.

I understood that this was not merely about choosing a partner; it was about acknowledging God in all my ways. The verse encouraged me to lay aside my fears and doubts and trust God to lead me. I realized that my understanding was limited, but God's wisdom was infinite. This Scripture became a cornerstone of my prayers and reflections during the fast, solidifying my resolve to seek God's will above all else.

10.2.3 Counsel from Elders

In addition to my personal prayer and fasting, I sought the counsel of wise elders in the faith. After the fast, I reached out to respected leaders within the UESI community. Their wisdom and experience in matters of marriage and relationships were invaluable.

When I shared my feelings about Rita and my desire to know God's will, they encouraged me, emphasizing the importance of seeking divine confirmation. They reminded me that marriage is a covenant before God and that it should be entered into with careful consideration and prayer. Their counsel provided me with assurance and comfort, reinforcing the belief that I was on the right path.

One elder mentioned, *"When God is in something, He will make it evident through various means."* This resonated with me, igniting a desire to look for signs and confirmations in my circumstances. I had already experienced a powerful sense of peace during my fast, and I now understood that this inner peace was a crucial indicator of God's leading.

10.2.4 External Circumstances

As I continued to pray, I paid close attention to

the external circumstances surrounding our budding relationship. Everything seemed to align perfectly: our families were supportive, and our shared faith and values were evident. I began to notice how naturally we complemented each other, both in our personalities and our spiritual journeys. It was as if God was weaving our paths together in a beautiful tapestry, and I felt a growing assurance that this was indeed His plan for us.

10.2.5 The Inner Peace

Amidst all these signs, the most compelling confirmation came from within—an overwhelming sense of inner peace. Even as I faced uncertainties and the challenges of navigating my future with Rita, I felt an unshakeable calm in my spirit. It was a peace that transcended understanding, a hallmark of God's presence in my life.

As I sought God in prayer, I experienced moments where I felt an affirmation of His love and guidance. This peace was not merely a fleeting emotion; it was a deep assurance that I was walking in alignment with God's will. I reflected on Philippians 4:6-7, which says, *"Do not be anxious about anything, but in every situation, by prayer and petition, with thanksgiving, present your requests to God. And the peace of God, which transcends all understanding, will guard your hearts and your minds in Christ Jesus. "*

This promise became a reality for me. Each time I prayed about Rita, I felt God's peace enveloping me, confirming that this proposal was indeed from Him. It was as if God was saying, "You are where I want you to be." This inner tranquility, coupled with the wisdom of my elders and the confirmation from Scripture, solidified my decision.

A Divine Conclusion

By the end of my fasting period and after seeking counsel from elders, I felt assured that my relationship with Rita was a divine orchestration. I came to a strong conviction that this proposal was from the Lord. I did not want to be swayed by external pressures or circumstances; I wanted to stand firm on the foundation of God's truth.

The convergence of the fasting experience, the counsel from elders, the supportive external circumstances, and the inner peace collectively affirmed that I was moving in the right direction. I recognized that marrying Rita was not just a personal decision but a part of God's greater plan for our lives. As I prepared to take the next steps in our relationship, I did so with a heart full of gratitude. I had sought God earnestly, and He had responded in ways that were clear and unmistakable. My journey of finding God's will in my marriage was a testament to His faithfulness, reminding me that when we seek Him wholeheartedly, He will guide our paths.

With a firm foundation built on prayer, fasting, and divine confirmation, I was ready to embark on the beautiful journey of marriage with Rita, trusting in God's perfect will for our lives together.

10.2.6 Divine Guidance

Over the next few weeks, spiritual leaders, mentors, and UESI elders became involved in our marriage talks. They approached the matter with prayer and wisdom, carefully guiding us both. It was a delicate process, but as 2 Timothy 1:7 reminds us, *"For the Spirit God gave us does not make us timid, but gives us power, love, and self-discipline."* This verse became a lifeline for me, reminding me that God's Spirit was guiding me, even in moments when I felt uncertain or fearful.

Now came the even greater challenge—convincing my parents. My family, deeply rooted in traditional Hindu beliefs, valued caste, dowry, and societal status above all else. I had seen how these values played out in my own mother's life, how she suffered in her marriage due to the dowry system and religious pride. I had long prayed that my own marriage would be different—that it would be built on spiritual values, mutual respect, and God's guidance.

Yet, convincing my parents was no easy task. The caste system was still very much a part of their worldview, and they held deeply entrenched beliefs about marriage. Rita came from Karnataka, and she was from a respectable family with a good education and Christian values, her background was not a big problem.

The dowry system was another factor. Even though I was against it, it still held sway in my family's decision-making process. The idea of giving or receiving a dowry was ingrained in the cultural consciousness, and any deviation from this could bring shame to the family. But as Ephesians 5:25 reminds us, *"Husbands, love your wives, just as Christ loved the church and gave himself up for her."* I believed that my marriage, like Christ's love for the church, should be founded on sacrifice, not material gain.

I knew that if I were to move forward with marrying Rita, I needed to navigate these complex social and cultural expectations with great care. My parents had to be convinced not only that Rita was a good match for me but also that this union was God-ordained. After many prayers, long discussions, and counsel from elders, my parents began to soften. Rita's education, character, and Christian faith gradually won them over. In time, they agreed to bless our union, though it wasn't without a struggle. I still remember my father saying, "She is a good girl, but are you sure?" It was a typical paternal concern, but eventually, my family accepted that this was God's will.

Both of our families were now involved in the marriage talks, and soon, it became an official arranged marriage with the blessings of our elders and relatives. It felt surreal how quickly everything had moved from a letter handed to me at the gates of UBS, Pune, to now, with both families coming together in unity.

But as with all things, there was still one

challenge left—finances. I had committed myself fully to ministry and UESI, and there was no single penny. Weddings in our culture often require large amounts of money for ceremonies, celebrations, and gifts. How would I afford all this? Once again, I found myself relying on God's provision. As Philippians 4:19 says, *"And my God will meet all your needs according to the riches of His glory in Christ Jesus."* I clung to this promise, knowing that God had led me this far and He would not abandon me now.

10.3 How I Got Married

In October 2002, the most pivotal moment in my life was set in motion—the day when the wedding talks between Rita and me were finalized. It was a moment that required not just my personal conviction but also the blessing of several people who were important to me. Along with my family, I was accompanied by UESI elders like Mr. Williams and Mr. Sunder Singh to Rita's home in Raichur. As the talks progressed, and both families agreed, we fixed the wedding date. While this should have been a moment of celebration, the reality of the financial demands that come with an Indian wedding weighed heavily on my heart.

I had no savings, and I was committed to living by faith. The idea of borrowing money or asking others for financial help didn't sit well with me. From the start, I resolved that my wedding would be a testimony of God's provision, not human effort. The costs associated with a traditional wedding seemed overwhelming, but I trusted that God would show me a way forward, as He had done in the past. It was around this time that a plan began to form in my mind.

10.3.1 Spiritual Life Conference at Paloncha

Well before my wedding date was fixed, a major regional-level spiritual conference was planned for January 2003 in Paloncha, Telangana. I was deeply involved in organizing the conference as part of my role as a field staff member with UESI. As the conference approached, the idea dawned on me: What if I got married on the last day of the conference? The logistics of the event would already be in place, a large gathering of godly people would already be there, and the cost of organizing a separate wedding would be significantly reduced.

This idea felt like a revelation, a solution

provided by God to address the resource challenge I faced. I couldn't stop thinking about how perfect it seemed. I imagined the conference concluding with my wedding as a beautiful, spiritually significant event. I took this idea in prayer, believing that God had placed it in my heart.

10.3.2 Seeking Approval and Facing Obstacles

With the idea in mind, I approached the UESI leadership, hoping they would agree. However, I quickly realized that it wasn't as simple as I had thought. The leaders pointed out that UESI, being a para-church organization, couldn't conduct a wedding ceremony during a conference. They felt that the event's purpose was solely spiritual and focused on evangelism and discipleship, not personal celebrations. I was disappointed. I had been so sure that this was God's answer to my prayer, but now it seemed that the door was closed. Doubts crept in—had I misunderstood God's direction? Was I being too idealistic in expecting everything to fall into place?

10.3.3 Ps Wilson & Ramakrishna's Support

Just when it seemed like my plan had failed, God intervened in an unexpected way. My beloved brother *Mr. Ramakrishna*, who had always been a source of support in my life, stepped in to help. He approached Pastor Wilson, a godly man who led a church directly across from the conference venue. Ramakrishna explained my situation and the financial burden I was facing.

To my great relief, Pastor Wilson graciously offered his church for the wedding, free of charge. His kindness was a clear answer to my prayers, and I saw God's hand at work in this provision. Now, the idea of getting married on the last day of the conference could be realized, not in the conference hall, but in a church nearby. This was an enormous weight lifted from my shoulders, and it reaffirmed my faith in God's provision. As the Bible says, "And my God will meet all your needs according to the riches of His glory in Christ Jesus" (Philippians 4:19).

10.3.4 Mr. Ezekiel's Generosity
Another pivotal figure during this time was *Mr. Ezekiel*, a senior graduate from Paloncha and a respected elder in the Christian community. When he learned about my situation, he stepped in like a father figure. He took on the responsibility of ensuring that the wedding would be organized smoothly,

coordinating with others, and overseeing many of the logistics.

His involvement was a tremendous blessing, especially since I was still immersed in managing the conference. I had to juggle both the conference responsibilities and wedding preparations, but with the help of people like Mr. Ezekiel, I was able to do so without feeling overwhelmed. His support, alongside others who volunteered their time and effort, was yet another reminder that when we place our trust in God, He sends the right people to help us along the way.

10.3.5 Simple Invitations and Minimal Costs

Due to the constraints of both time and resources, my wedding planning took on an air of simplicity. I spent a meager Rs. 100 (about $1.20) on printing a few wedding cards to distribute among key leaders at the conference. For everyone else, the invitation was extended verbally. This was unconventional, especially in a culture where formal invitations are a must, but I trusted that God would bring the right people to witness our union.

The simplicity of the arrangements mirrored the simplicity of my life and faith. There were no grandiose wedding cards or expensive decorations. Instead, it was a humble affair, reflecting the deeper significance of what was happening—a covenant made before God and in the company of His people.

Rita and her family arrived on a hired bus just an hour before the wedding ceremony. There were no private rooms or special accommodations, and yet, despite these material limitations, the atmosphere was filled with joy and peace. It was a reminder that weddings are not about grandeur but about the spiritual union being formed.

10.3.6 The Wedding Day: Attire and Decorations

With all the focus on the conference, I hadn't given much thought to my own wedding attire. I was still wearing my old clothes from the conference when some of my Warangal EU students approached me with a gift—a new pair of pants and a shirt. They had bought these clothes for me as their wedding gift. It was a simple gesture, but one that touched my heart deeply. I saw this as yet another way in which God was providing for me, even in the small details.

Just as I was about to head to the church, Mr. Ezekiel stopped me. He asked, "Where is your suit?" I told him I didn't have one, and without hesitation, he took me to his house. He brought out his own wedding suit, which had been stored away for years. Although it was old, it fit me perfectly, and I wore it with deep gratitude, knowing that God had provided it once again.

Similarly, the wedding decorations were handled with the same faith-driven simplicity. I handed Rs. 100 (about $1.20) to Jaipaul, one of the Paloncha EU students, and asked him to use it for decorating the church. I wasn't sure how far that small amount would go, but to my surprise, the church looked beautiful. It wasn't lavish, but it was perfect for the occasion. It reminded me of how Jesus multiplied the loaves and fishes, turning what little we had into something more than enough (Matthew 14:19-21).

10.3.7 The Flower Bouquet

Even on my wedding day, there was one more need that I hadn't anticipated. As Rita was about to enter the church, I realized she didn't have a bouquet of flowers to hold, as was customary. My heart sank for

a moment, but God, in His wisdom, had already prepared a solution.

My Warangal GGF lady graduates—Mrs.

Saraswathi, Mrs. Olivia, and Mrs. Alpha Anandraj—noticed the missing bouquet and immediately acted. They rushed to the church garden, picked some natural flowers, and quickly crafted a bouquet for Rita. The result was a beautiful, natural bouquet, more elegant than anything store-bought. The flowers looked fresh, vibrant, and perfect in Rita's hands, a true testament to how God's provision is always timely and abundant.

10.3.8 A Grand Spiritual Celebration

The wedding ceremony itself was a deeply spiritual and joyous event. I am ever grateful to Pastor Wilson for his amazing support in organizing the entire day. The service was graced by the presence of Mr. Williams and Mr. Vilbert, who both gave their heartfelt blessings. Mrs. Gladys, a senior UESI staff member from Karnataka and the speaker at the conference blessed our wedding with a powerful sermon. Her words not only encouraged us but also filled the entire ceremony with a sense of divine purpose.

The atmosphere was one of profound joy and spiritual depth. Everyone present could sense that this was more than just a wedding—it was a divine appointment. God had brought everything together in ways that no human effort could have accomplished. The entire day reflected His glory, from the people who participated to the spiritual richness that filled the church.

10.3.9 The Journey Continues

Looking back, I can say with confidence that our wedding was truly a *"**grandeur**"* and Spirit-filled time. Every detail, from the suit I wore to the bouquet Rita held, was a testimony of God's faithfulness. All those present blessed us abundantly, and their prayers carried us forward into our married life.

The rest, as they say, is history. Our marriage, built on the foundation of God's provision and grace, has been a journey of blessings, challenges, and growth. Through it all, we have seen the hand of Almighty God guiding and sustaining us, and for that, we are ever grateful.

This chapter, *The Struggle of Resources*, not only highlights the financial challenges I faced but, more importantly, it testifies to God's miraculous provision in every moment leading up to and during our wedding day. From a simple wedding plan emerged a celebration filled with the Spirit of God and a community of believers.

Conclusion

As I reflect on my journey in *Echoes of Eternity: Bhakta Potana's Spiritual Awakening*, I see not only a story of personal transformation but also the powerful impact of family, faith, and global ministry. The narrative I've shared so far is a testament to God's grace, His divine orchestration of my life, and His presence through every challenge and victory. However, the story doesn't end here. This conclusion serves to introduce the continuation of the narrative, which involves not only my ministry and academic pursuits but also the significant influence of my family, as well as the many travels that have shaped my global perspective.

Family Impact: The Role of Sophia, Lydia, and Ashish

At the core of my life and ministry is my family—my children, who have been both a source of strength and a reflection of God's blessings. Each of them has impacted my journey in unique ways, and they represent the continuation of the spiritual legacy I hope to leave behind. Our family has remained steadfast in our faith through the power of family prayer, which continues to be our strength in every season of life.

Sophia: A Gift of Intellectual Brilliance

Sophia, my eldest daughter, was born in Raichur at a time when life was filled with both challenges and promise. From her earliest years, it was evident that she had been gifted with an incredible intellect. She possessed a natural curiosity about the world and an eagerness to learn, which quickly set her apart. As she grew, her academic achievements and intellectual prowess became a defining characteristic, and we could see God's hand in her development.

Sophia's intellectual journey has been marked by perseverance and excellence. Today, she is pursuing her studies at Hardin-Simmons University (HSU) in Abilene, Texas, USA. Her achievements are a reflection of her dedication, and we, as her parents, take pride not only in her academic success but also in her spiritual growth. A significant moment in Sophia's spiritual journey was when she accepted the Lord and was born again. I had the immense privilege of giving her the immersion baptism, marking her public declaration of faith in Jesus Christ. Sophia's presence at HSU is a testament to the value of faith-driven education, where intellectual inquiry and spiritual formation go hand in hand. Her future is bright, and I am confident that God has great plans for her as she continues to use her gifts to serve Him.

Lydia: The Joy of a Second Gift
Lydia, our second daughter, was born during our time of ministry in the lower hills of the Himalayas. Like her sister, Lydia has demonstrated an extraordinary intellect and a passion for learning from a young age. The unique setting of her birth—a place known for its spirituality and natural beauty—seemed

to imbue her with a sense of purpose and brilliance that has only grown with time.

Lydia's education has been a priority, and today she is studying at Northern Marianas College (NMC) in Saipan, USA, where she lives with us. She has thrived in her studies, and her intellectual curiosity continues to inspire those around her. More importantly, Lydia, too, has accepted the Lord into her life and experienced the transformative power of being born again. Like Sophia, I had the privilege of baptizing Lydia by immersion, a deeply meaningful moment in our family's spiritual journey. Watching both Sophia and Lydia grow into capable and thoughtful young women has been one of the greatest joys of my life. As they pursue their respective academic paths, I am reminded of the importance of nurturing both mind and spirit, and I am grateful to see how God has worked through them.

Ashish: The Promised Child

Ashish, my son, was born during a significant chapter of my life—during the time I was pursuing my PhD at SAIACS in Bangalore. His arrival felt like the fulfillment of a promise, a gift from God that brought incredible joy and completion to our family. As the youngest of my children, Ashish holds a special place in our hearts, and his presence has been a constant reminder of God's faithfulness.

Watching Ashish grow has been a blessing. His birth, during such a pivotal time in my academic and spiritual journey, felt like a divine affirmation of the path I was on. As he matures, I am excited to see how God will use him, just as He has guided his sisters. Ashish's life is a testament to God's perfect timing and the ways in which He blesses us, often in unexpected moments.

Ministry in the Lower Himalayas
A Place of Blessing and Family Growth
Our ministry in the lower hills of the Himalayas in Uttarakhand was one of the most spiritually fulfilling and transformative periods of my life. The isolation of the region, coupled with the beauty of the mountains, created an environment ripe for deep spiritual reflection and ministry. Ministering to the communities in this area, who lived simple yet spiritually rich lives, was a reminder of how the Gospel can take root even in the most remote places.

It was during this period that God blessed us with Lydia, whose birth in the Himalayas marked a new chapter in our family life. The challenges of raising a family in such a remote location were significant, but the rewards far outweighed them. The community around us became an extended family, and the simplicity of life allowed for a deeper connection with God. This time not only strengthened my ministry but also reinforced the importance of family in the context of God's work.

As a father, I sought to instill in my children the values of faith, perseverance, and intellectual curiosity. The lessons we learned in the Himalayas—about community, sacrifice, and God's provision—have stayed with us and continue to shape our family's journey. The ministry work in this region, though difficult, laid a foundation for future opportunities and opened doors for global outreach.

Academic Pursuits
Building a Foundation for Ministry
My academic journey has been marked by a pursuit of theological and philosophical knowledge that has enriched both my personal faith and my ministry. Each degree, from the Th.M. at Union

Biblical Seminary (UBS) in Pune to the MA in Religion and Philosophy at Madurai Kamaraj University (MKU) in Tamil Nadu, has provided me with the tools to engage deeply with the intellectual and spiritual challenges of ministry.

Th.M. at UBS, Pune

My time at UBS was transformative, not just academically but spiritually. It was here that I developed a deeper understanding of missiology and how the Gospel can be contextualized in diverse cultural settings. The theological training, I received at UBS provided the foundation for much of my later ministry work. The seminary's emphasis on academic rigor and spiritual formation prepared me for the complex challenges I would face in my future ministry roles.

The relationships I built at UBS, both with faculty and fellow students, were instrumental in shaping my approach to ministry. These connections have continued to influence my work, as many of the people I met during my time at UBS have gone on to serve in significant leadership roles in the global church.

MA (Religion & Philosophy) at MKU

The decision to pursue an MA in Religion and Philosophy at MKU was driven by a desire to understand the broader philosophical underpinnings of religious belief. This degree allowed me to explore the intersections of faith, culture, and reason, and it provided a framework for engaging with people of other faiths in a respectful and informed manner.

Studying religion and philosophy in an academic setting expanded my intellectual horizons and deepened my understanding of the human search for meaning. The insights I gained from this program have been invaluable in my ministry, particularly in interfaith contexts where dialogue and mutual understanding are essential.

MSW at Acharya Nagarjuna University

In addition to my theological studies, I pursued a Master of Social Work (MSW) at Acharya Nagarjuna University (ANU) in Guntur. This program equipped me with practical skills for addressing the social and economic challenges faced by the communities I served. The MSW program reinforced the idea that ministry must extend beyond the spiritual realm and address the material needs of people as well.

The social work training I received has been instrumental in my ministry, particularly in areas of community development and outreach. Whether it was working with marginalized communities or providing support to individuals facing personal crises, the MSW degree gave me the tools to serve more effectively and compassionately.

Global Travels
Expanding Ministry Beyond Borders

One of the most profound aspects of my ministry has been the opportunity to travel across the globe, sharing the Gospel and teaching in various cultural contexts. These travels have not only enriched my personal understanding of global Christianity but have also allowed me to build connections with believers from diverse backgrounds.

Visiting Sri Lanka

One of the early highlights of my global ministry was attending the International Fellowship of Evangelical Students (IFES) conference in Sri Lanka. This experience was eye-opening, as it provided a platform to engage with Christian leaders from around the world. The discussions at the conference highlighted the shared challenges faced by Christians globally and reinforced the importance of student ministry in shaping future leaders.

The connections I made during the IFES conference have continued to influence my work as I collaborate with fellow leaders to strengthen student ministries across borders. Sri Lanka, with its unique religious landscape, provided a fascinating context for these discussions, and the insights I gained during this trip have stayed with me.

Preaching and Teaching in the USA

Since 2012, I have been privileged to visit the United States every year, where I engage in teaching and preaching ministry across various states. Each year, I travel to different parts of the country, sharing God's word with diverse congregations. These visits have been an incredible blessing, as they have allowed me to witness firsthand the global reach of Christianity. From Texas to New York, Georgia to California, my travels in the USA have deepened my appreciation for the diversity of the global church. Each state has its unique cultural and spiritual landscape, and I have been fortunate to engage with congregations that are passionate about their faith and eager to grow in their understanding of scripture.

These annual visits have provided opportunities for fellowship, teaching, and spiritual renewal. The relationships I have built with churches and individuals across the USA have enriched my ministry and broadened my understanding of how God is at work in different cultural contexts.

Ministry in Seoul
South Korea: A Month of Teaching and Preaching

Another significant global experience was my month-long trip to Seoul City, South Korea, where I engaged in teaching and preaching ministry. South Korea is known for its vibrant Christian community, and my time there was a reminder of how the Gospel transcends cultural boundaries. The dedication of the Korean church to prayer, worship, and community engagement was inspiring, and it was an honor to be part of their spiritual journey.

The time I spent in Seoul it was allowed me to explore how the Gospel is lived out in a context that blends traditional Korean values with modern expressions of faith. It was a privilege to contribute to the spiritual growth of the people I met there, and the experience deepened my appreciation for the global body of Christ.

Visits to Dubai
Presenting Scholarly Papers and Engaging in Ministry

During my PhD studies, I had the opportunity to visit Dubai multiple times to present scholarly papers and engage in ministry work. Dubai, with its large expatriate population, provided a unique context for ministry, and I was able to connect with Christians from various cultural backgrounds.

Presenting scholarly papers at *Heriot-Watt Dubai University* and participating in teaching and preaching ministries in Dubai broadened my academic and ministerial horizons. The diverse Christian community in Dubai provided a rich environment for learning and collaboration, and my time there reinforced the importance of global partnerships in ministry.

Ministry in Nepal
Engaging with the Christian Community in the Hills

Every year, I have had the privilege of traveling to Nepal to teach at the Nepal National Christian College (NNCC) in East Nepal. These visits have been an important part of my ministry as I engage with students and pastors in the hills of Nepal. Teaching in Nepal has been a unique experience, as the Christian community there is relatively small but growing.

The students and pastors I have worked with in Nepal are passionate about their faith and eager to learn. My time in Nepal has been a reminder of the global nature of God's mission and the importance of supporting Christian leaders in every context. The hills of Nepal, much like the Himalayas in Uttarakhand, have become a place of spiritual growth and transformation for both the people I serve and myself.

India Mission Bible School, Karimnagar
Teaching Part-Time

During my time in Hyderabad, I took on the role of a part-time instructor at the India Mission Bible School in Karimnagar. This position allowed me to engage with students who were eager to deepen their understanding of Scripture and grow in their faith. Teaching on Saturdays provided a valuable opportunity to connect with individuals preparing for ministry in various contexts.

At the India Mission Bible School, I taught courses on Church History, Theology, and Christian

Ethics, focusing on equipping students with the theological foundations they would need in their ministries. The experience of teaching was immensely fulfilling, as I witnessed students grappling with theological concepts, applying them to their lives, and developing a clearer sense of their calling. The classroom became a space for open dialogue, where students shared their insights and experiences, enriching the learning environment for everyone involved.

This role reinforced my belief in the importance of theological education and its impact on effective ministry. It was a privilege to mentor leaders and witness their growth as they prepared to serve in their ministry. The relationships formed during this time have continued to be a source of encouragement.

Caleb Institute, New Delhi
Teaching Th.M. Students

My teaching journey extended to the Caleb Institute in New Delhi, where I had the opportunity to instruct Th.M. students in advanced theological concepts. Teaching at Caleb Institute was particularly enriching, as it allowed me to engage with a diverse group of students from various backgrounds and contexts.

The courses I taught included Biblical Theology of Missions, Theologies of Mission, and The Gospel and Culture. These subjects are crucial for any aspiring theologian and ministry leader, as they provide the framework for understanding the complexities of the contemporary world through a biblical lens. My goal was to challenge students to think critically and apply their theological training to real-world situations. Working with Th.M. students at Caleb was not just an academic endeavor; it was also a deeply spiritual experience. Students came with their own questions, struggles, and aspirations, and it was a privilege to guide them in their quest for deeper understanding. The interactions and discussions we had enriched my own faith and helped me refine my teaching approach, making it more relevant and impactful.

COTR, Bheemili, Visakhapatnam
Teaching Th.M. Students

In addition to my work at Hyderabad, I also taught courses to Th.M. students at COTR (Church on the Rock Theological Seminary) in Bhimili, Visakapatnam. This role allowed me to further engage with students who were dedicated to pursuing advanced theological education and preparing for ministry.

At COTR, I taught courses on the History of Christianity, Biblical Theology of Missions, and Theologies of Mission. My aim was to equip students with the necessary skills to effectively lead congregations and engage in community outreach. I emphasized the importance of integrating theological knowledge with practical application, ensuring that students understood the relevance of their studies in real-world ministry contexts.

The teaching experience at COTR was not only about imparting knowledge but also about fostering a supportive community of learners. Many of the students were actively involved in local churches, and our discussions often centered around their real-life challenges and opportunities. Being part of their academic journey and witnessing their growth as leaders was incredibly fulfilling.

Establishing the COACH
Institute of Intercultural Studies

During the COVID-19 pandemic, I saw an opportunity to leverage technology to reach students who were seeking theological education and training from home. This led to the establishment of the COACH Institute of Intercultural Studies, an online Bible school designed to provide accessible theological education to a global audience.

The online format allowed me to reach individuals from various countries and backgrounds, creating a diverse learning environment. The curriculum focused on intercultural studies, contextual theology, and practical ministry skills, empowering students to engage with their communities effectively. The COACH Institute quickly became a blessing to many, providing resources and training during a time when in-person gatherings were limited.

Students enrolled in the program benefited from live lectures, interactive discussions, and access to a wealth of online resources. The response to the institute was overwhelmingly positive, and it became clear that the need for theological education in an online format was significant. Establishing the COACH Institute was one of the most rewarding experiences of my ministry, as it allowed me to contribute to the spiritual formation of many who were eager to learn and grow.

Mission Activities in Hyderabad
Pastors Training, Evangelistic Activities, Camps, and Conferences

While based in Hyderabad, I was also involved in various mission activities beyond teaching. I organized and participated in training sessions for pastors, evangelistic outreach events, and spiritual camps and conferences that aimed to equip and encourage church leaders and laypeople alike.

The pastors' training sessions focused on practical skills and theological knowledge, addressing the unique challenges faced by church leaders in the region. These sessions provided a platform for pastors to share their experiences, learn from one another, and receive guidance on effective ministry practices. It was a joy to see the camaraderie that developed among the participants, as they supported each other in their respective ministries.

In addition to training, I also organized evangelistic activities aimed at reaching those who had not yet heard the Gospel. These outreach events allowed us to connect with local communities, share testimonies, and present the message of Christ in a compelling way. The excitement and enthusiasm of those participating were infectious, and witnessing lives transformed by the Gospel reinforced my commitment to mission work.

Camps and conferences provided opportunities for spiritual renewal and encouragement. They brought together individuals from various backgrounds to worship, learn, and grow in their faith. I had the privilege of teaching at several of these events, and seeing attendees encounter God in profound ways was a reminder of the importance of community in the faith journey.

My Stay at EI, Greenville

From September 1, 2023, to January 10, 2024, I had the privilege of staying at the Evangelical Institute (EI) in Greenville, South Carolina. This time at EI was an immensely important chapter in my life, one that I now reflect on as a season of spiritual rejuvenation and preparation. After years of extensive ministry—teaching, preaching, and traveling across the globe—I found myself in need of rest and renewal, and EI provided just that. It was not only a retreat from the busyness of ministry but also a time of deep spiritual nurturing that reinvigorated my soul.

In many ways, my stay at EI felt like a sabbatical, offering me the opportunity to reconnect with God on a personal level, away from the constant demands of ministry. During this time, I was able to step back and reflect on the past years, and through prayer, worship, and study, I sensed God ministering to me in new and profound ways. After the physical and mental exhaustion of years of intensive travel and teaching, EI became a sanctuary where I could rest in God's presence and receive the spiritual nourishment I desperately needed. It was a time of healing, reflection, and renewal—a sacred pause that allowed me to focus on my relationship with God.

One of the highlights of my time at EI was the opportunity to take several spiritual courses, which greatly enriched my faith. These courses were not only intellectually stimulating but also deeply transformative, helping me to rediscover the joy of studying God's Word in a focused, reflective environment. I felt God preparing and equipping me for greater ministry during this time. The insights I gained from these courses have not only deepened my own spiritual life but have also provided fresh perspectives that I will carry forward in my future ministry endeavors. I could feel God shaping my heart and mind, readying me for the next chapter of service He has prepared for me.

In addition to the spiritual nourishment I received, my time at EI was also incredibly productive. I was deeply engaged in a writing project to publish academic textbooks on missiology, which had been on my heart for some time. Every moment at EI was precious, and I used every available minute to write, pouring my thoughts and research into these academic works. This period of focused writing allowed me to consolidate years of experience and study into comprehensive textbooks that I hope will serve as valuable resources for theological students and ministry leaders alike. The environment at EI provided the perfect backdrop for this project, with its peaceful atmosphere and the presence of God so tangible around me.

During this time, another remarkable event unfolded—my transition from EI to my new role as

Professor of Theology at EUCON in Saipan. This transition was nothing short of miraculous. It was a smooth and divinely orchestrated process, one that reaffirmed my faith in God's perfect timing and provision. What could have been a stressful and uncertain transition turned out to be seamless, and I give all the glory to God for guiding me through it. The shift from EI to EUCON marked the beginning of a new season in my ministry, and I am excited to see how God will continue to use me in this new role.

My stay at EI will forever be remembered as a time of spiritual refreshment, personal growth, and preparation for the greater things God has in store for me. It was a period that reaffirmed the importance of rest and reflection in the life of a minister, and I left EI feeling equipped and ready to embrace the next phase of my calling.

My Publications
A Journey of Faith and Scholarship

Throughout my life, writing has been a significant avenue through which I have been able to express the theological insights, missiological experiences, and spiritual lessons that God has graciously imparted to me. I have had the privilege of authoring several books and scholarly articles, all of which reflect my deep commitment to advancing the Gospel and fostering a deeper understanding of God's mission in the world. Each publication represents not only years of research, study, and ministry experience but also a deep reliance on God's grace and wisdom. I give all the glory to God, as these works are a testament to His guidance and provision in my life.

One of my early works, *New Testament Themes*, explores the central theological themes found in the New Testament. This book is designed to help readers better understand the teachings of Jesus and the apostles, offering a comprehensive overview of key concepts such as salvation, grace, faith, and the kingdom of God. Similarly, my book *Old Testament Themes* provides an in-depth study of the foundational theological themes in the Old Testament, including covenant, prophecy, law, and redemption. Both of these works have been invaluable resources for students of theology and ministry, helping them grasp the richness and depth of the biblical narrative.

In my book *Witnessing to Tribals: Efficacy of COUNT in Indian Missions*, I explore the unique challenges and opportunities of evangelizing tribal communities in India. Drawing from my own experience in ministry, this book highlights the importance of contextualization and cultural sensitivity when sharing the Gospel with indigenous peoples. Similarly, *Tribals in India: An Anthropo-Missiological Perspective* provides a more academic look at the anthropological and missiological aspects of reaching tribal populations, offering insights into their cultures, beliefs, and practices, and how these factors influence mission strategies.

My interest in theological education and missiology led to the publication of *Theological Themes Volume 1*, a compilation of essays and studies on key theological concepts, and *Missiological Themes: An Asian Perspective on Christian Mission and Praxis*, published in two volumes. These books address the critical issues of mission work in Asia, exploring how the Gospel can be contextualized in different cultural settings and examining the praxis of mission in an increasingly globalized world. By focusing on the Asian context, these works provide valuable insights for anyone involved in mission work in this region, offering practical strategies and theological reflections that are grounded in local realities.

One of the most heartfelt projects I have undertaken is *Shadows of the Street: India's Street Children*, a book that addresses the plight of homeless children in India. This work shines a light on the often-overlooked issue of street children, offering both a theological and practical framework for how the church can respond to this urgent need. It is a call to action for the Christian community to engage in social justice and mercy ministries, particularly for vulnerable and marginalized populations.

In *Indigenous Missions in India*, I explore the role of local, indigenous mission movements in India and how they differ from traditional Western mission models. This book is a tribute to the many men and women in India who are serving their communities with the Gospel, often in the face of significant challenges and opposition. It also highlights the importance of empowering local leaders to take ownership of the mission in their own cultural contexts, a theme that is increasingly relevant in today's global mission landscape.

Campus Ministry: A Contextualized Approach is another significant work that focuses on the importance of engaging with young adults in the university setting. This book offers a practical guide for campus ministers, providing strategies for reaching students with the Gospel in a way that is relevant to their unique social and intellectual environment. As someone who has spent many years in student ministry, this book represents my heart for the next generation of Christian leaders and my desire to see them grounded in their faith during a crucial time in their lives.

Christian Missions Historiography: An Indian Perspective offers a historical analysis of Christian mission efforts in India, highlighting the contributions of both Western and indigenous missionaries. This work provides an Indian perspective on the history of missions, offering a balanced view that acknowledges both the successes and challenges of missionary work in the subcontinent. It is a valuable resource for anyone interested in the history of Christianity in India and the development of mission movements over the centuries. Finally, I am particularly proud of *Echoes of Eternity: Bhakta Potana's Spiritual Awakening*, the autobiography that chronicles my own spiritual journey. This book is not merely a recounting of personal experiences but is meant to encourage readers to trust in the Lord and witness the power of His transforming grace. My life, as documented in this book, is a testament to God's faithfulness, and I give all the glory to Him for everything that has been accomplished. This work, like all of my other publications, is intended to point people to Christ and inspire them to live out their faith with boldness and conviction.

In addition to these books, I have also published numerous scholarly articles in international journals, contributing to the ongoing dialogue in theology, missiology, and ministry practices. These articles address a wide range of topics, from biblical studies to mission strategies, and have been an important part of my academic and ministerial contribution to the global church.

All of these publications have been made possible by God's grace alone. Each book and article is the result of His wisdom, strength, and guidance in my life. My prayer is that these works will continue to bless, equip, and encourage others in their own spiritual journeys. As I reflect on these accomplishments, I am reminded that they are not my achievements but are the Lord's. To Him belongs all the glory, honor, and praise.

EUCON, Saipan, USA

Present Ministry as Professor of Theology

Today, I continue to serve as a Professor of Theology at EUCON International University in Saipan, USA. This role allows me to engage with students from diverse cultural backgrounds, providing theological education in a global context. Teaching at EUCON has been a rewarding experience, as I see students grow in their understanding of scripture and theology, preparing them for ministry in their own communities.

My time in Saipan has been a continuation of my commitment to global ministry, and it has been a blessing to be part of the EUCON community. The students I teach come from different parts of the world, and it is a privilege to contribute to their spiritual and academic growth.

In penning *Echoes of Eternity: Bhakta Potana's Spiritual Awakening*, I seek not to exalt myself but to give all glory to God for the remarkable journey He has orchestrated in my life. Each chapter, marked by trials and triumphs, is a testament to His unwavering faithfulness and grace. It is through His divine guidance that I have experienced transformation, fulfillment, and purpose, and I hope that my story serves as an encouragement to readers everywhere. Trusting the Lord has been the cornerstone of my journey, and it is my prayer that those who read these pages will be inspired to place their faith in Him, knowing that He is capable of achieving far more than we can ask or imagine. All the achievements and milestones documented here are not mine but are a reflection of God's love and provision, and I give Him all the praise and honor for what He has done in my life.

Introduction to Volume 2

As we reach the conclusion of *Echoes of Eternity: Bhakta Potana's Spiritual Awakening*, it is important to recognize that this is not the end of the story but rather a bridge to the next volume. The journey chronicled in this first volume has been filled with divine encounters, challenges, and personal transformation. However, God's work in my life continues, and the following pages have only scratched the surface of the many blessings, lessons, and ministry opportunities that He has unfolded for me. Volume 2 of this autobiography will provide a deeper and more expansive exploration of the various aspects of my life, family, and ministry that I've been privileged to experience. This volume will focus on how God has continued to shape and guide my journey, particularly through my work in the Himalayas, my academic pursuits, my global travels, and the ministries He has called me to lead.

The upcoming volume will offer readers an opportunity to witness the fullness of God's grace and provision in ways that have profoundly impacted my personal life, my family, and the communities I have served. As I continue to reflect on the milestones of my ministry and the academic foundations that have supported my work, Volume 2 will document not only the highlights of these experiences but also the spiritual growth that has accompanied them. It is my hope that this next volume will not only inspire readers to see God's hand at work in every aspect of their lives but also encourage them to continue their own journeys of faith, trusting in God's guidance and provision at every step.

Ministry in the Lower Himalayas: A Place of Blessing and Family Growth

One of the most significant seasons of my life, which will be elaborated in Volume 2, is my ministry in the lower Himalayas. This period was marked by both spiritual growth and family blessings. The lower Himalayas, with their majestic peaks and remote communities, became a place of profound transformation for me and my family. It was here that I truly came to understand the depth of God's calling on my life. Ministering in such a rugged and isolated region presented unique challenges, yet it was precisely through these challenges that I experienced some of the greatest blessings.

During my time in the Himalayas, I witnessed firsthand how the simplicity of life in these remote villages created a space for deep spiritual engagement.

The people I ministered to were hungry for the Gospel, and I was privileged to see lives transformed by the message of Christ. At the same time, this season was also a time of great personal blessing for my family. It was in this setting that our second daughter, Lydia, was born, a gift that served as a constant reminder of God's grace and provision. Volume 2 will provide a deeper exploration of how our family thrived during this time and how God used these experiences to shape the future direction of our ministry.

Academic Pursuits: Building a Foundation for Ministry

A key theme in Volume 2 will be the role of academic pursuits in shaping my ministry and understanding of theology. Throughout my life, I have placed a high value on education, recognizing that theological study provides the necessary tools to engage with the world in a meaningful and effective way. In Volume 2, I will delve into how my academic journey has been a cornerstone of my ministry and how each degree I pursued contributed to my spiritual growth and leadership development.

Th.M. at Union Biblical Seminary (UBS), Pune

One of the foundational academic experiences that will be explored in detail is my time at Union Biblical Seminary (UBS) in Pune, where I earned a Master of Theology (Th.M.). This program provided a comprehensive theological education, allowing me to engage with advanced concepts in missiology, biblical studies, and practical theology. My time at UBS was transformative, not only because of the academic rigor but also because of the spiritual growth it facilitated. I will reflect on how the relationships I formed with professors and fellow students at UBS shaped my theological understanding and prepared me for the challenges of ministry in a complex, multicultural world.

The Th.M. at UBS helped solidify my calling to missions, and the academic training I received equipped me to serve in a more effective and contextualized way. In Volume 2, I will explore how specific courses and mentorship experiences at UBS impacted my approach to ministry and how these lessons have continued to influence my work over the years.

MA in Religion & Philosophy at Madurai Kamaraj University (MKU)

In addition to my theological studies, my pursuit of an MA in Religion and Philosophy at Madurai Kamaraj University (MKU) played a critical role in shaping my intellectual and spiritual development. This program allowed me to explore the intersections of faith, reason, and culture, providing a philosophical framework for engaging with people of diverse religious backgrounds. Volume 2 will dive into the impact this degree had on my ministry, particularly in the areas of interfaith dialogue and contextual theology.

Studying religion and philosophy broadened my understanding of how different worldviews influence individual and collective belief systems. In Volume 2, I will reflect on how these academic insights enabled me to engage more effectively with people from different cultural and religious contexts, particularly in regions like India where multiple faith traditions coexist. This degree was instrumental in helping me articulate a clear and compassionate approach to sharing the Gospel with those who hold different beliefs.

MSW at Acharya Nagarjuna University

The third academic pursuit that will be elaborated in Volume 2 is my Master of Social Work (MSW) degree from Acharya Nagarjuna University. This degree allowed me to integrate practical social work with my theological training, equipping me to serve the physical, emotional, and spiritual needs of the communities I ministered to. The MSW program provided the tools and knowledge needed to address issues like poverty, social injustice, and community development from a faith-based perspective.

In Volume 2, I will explore how my social work training helped shape my ministry's holistic approach. Whether I was engaging with street children, tribal communities, or local congregations, the skills I gained through my MSW degree allowed me to offer more comprehensive and effective solutions to the challenges these groups faced. This experience also deepened my understanding of the intersection between social service and evangelism, emphasizing the importance of addressing both spiritual and material needs.

Global Travels: Expanding Ministry Beyond Borders

Another key aspect of Volume 2 will be my global travels, which have significantly expanded the reach and impact of my ministry. Over the years, I have had the privilege of traveling to various countries to preach, teach, and participate in international conferences. These experiences have not only broadened my perspective on global Christianity but have also provided opportunities to connect with fellow believers and ministry leaders from diverse cultural backgrounds.

In Volume 2, I will elaborate on my travels to places like South Korea, where I spent a month teaching and preaching in Seoul City, and my annual trips to the United States, where I have preached and taught in multiple states, including Texas, California, and New York. Each of these trips has been a unique opportunity to witness how God is at work in different parts of the world, and I will share stories of how these experiences have enriched my understanding of global missions and the universal nature of the Gospel.

Additionally, I will explore the significance of my visits to Dubai, where I presented scholarly papers and engaged in ministry with expatriate communities. These international experiences have been transformative, providing new insights into the challenges and opportunities of cross-cultural ministry. Volume 2 will also reflect on the relationships and partnerships that have emerged from these travels, emphasizing the importance of collaboration in advancing God's mission across borders.

Teaching Ministry: National and International Seminaries

Teaching has always been a central part of my calling, and Volume 2 will provide an in-depth look at my teaching ministry in various national and international seminaries. Over the years, I have had the privilege of teaching students from diverse cultural and theological backgrounds, equipping them to become effective leaders in their own contexts. Volume 2 will expand on my experiences teaching at institutions like Caleb Institute in New Delhi and COTR Theological Seminary in Bhimili, Visakhapatnam, where I taught courses on missiology, biblical interpretation, and practical theology.

I will reflect on how these teaching opportunities allowed me to mentor future Christian leaders and how my own faith was strengthened through my interactions with students. Teaching in both national and international settings has provided me with a unique perspective on the challenges and opportunities facing the global church, and Volume 2 will explore how these experiences have shaped my approach to ministry and theological education.

Establishing the COACH: Institute of Intercultural Studies

One of the most significant initiatives I undertook during the COVID-19 pandemic was the establishment of the COACH: Institute of Intercultural Studies, an online Bible school designed to provide theological education to students around the world. Volume 2 will provide a detailed account of how this institute came into being and the impact it has had on students from diverse cultural backgrounds.

The COACH Institute was born out of a desire to continue providing theological training despite the limitations imposed by the pandemic. In Volume 2, I will share how God guided me through the process of establishing this online platform, and how the institute quickly became a blessing to many who were eager to learn and grow in their faith. The institute has allowed me to reach students from regions that would otherwise be difficult to access, and it has provided a space for cross-cultural dialogue and learning. Volume 2 will highlight the success stories of students who have benefited from the COACH Institute and how this initiative has expanded my ministry beyond geographical boundaries.

Mission Activities in Hyderabad: Pastors Training, Evangelistic Activities, Camps, and Conferences

Another key focus of Volume 2 will be the mission activities I engaged in while based in Hyderabad. These activities included training sessions for pastors, evangelistic outreach events, and spiritual camps and conferences aimed at equipping local church leaders and laypeople. Volume 2 will provide a detailed account of how these initiatives impacted the local Christian community and how God used these events to strengthen the faith of many.

I will also share testimonies from the pastors and lay leaders who participated in these training sessions, reflecting on how they were able to apply the lessons learned in their own ministries. The evangelistic activities, camps, and conferences were moments of spiritual renewal and encouragement, and

Volume 2 will offer a deeper exploration of how these events contributed to the growth and vitality of the Christian community in Hyderabad.

Pray and Prepare for Volume 2

As you reach the end of *Echoes of Eternity: Bhakta Potana's Spiritual Awakening*, I encourage you to pray and prepare for the lessons, stories, and insights that will be shared in *Volume 2*. This upcoming volume will offer a more comprehensive look at the various aspects of my ministry, academic pursuits, and global travels, providing readers with a deeper understanding of God's ongoing work in my life. It is my prayer that *Volume 2* will continue to inspire and encourage you to trust in God's faithfulness, just as I have experienced it throughout my journey. May God guide and bless you as you await the next volume, and may His grace continue to strengthen and sustain you in every season of life.

Books by this Author: Dr. Venkat Potana

Explore a range of books by this author, covering various themes and genres. All titles are available for purchase online through Amazon.com, making it easy to add them to your collection with just a few clicks.n

1. Echoes of Eternity: Bhakta Potana's Spiritual Awakening

Echoes of Eternity: Bhakta Potana's Spiritual Awakening" is a deeply personal and transformative journey of faith, set against the backdrop of a rich Hindu heritage and cultural traditions. Through this autobiography, Dr. Venkat Potana shares the profound experiences that shaped his life, from a childhood marked by hardship and spiritual longing to an eventual encounter with the living Christ that forever changed his destiny.

Raised amidst the tension of Vaishnavite and Shaivite religious practices, the author navigates the complexities of ancestral legacies, family conflicts, and personal struggles. The narrative captures his early years spent searching for meaning and divine intervention, culminating in a miraculous vision of Almighty God that redefined his understanding of faith, purpose, and peace. With vivid memories of family, tradition, and spiritual battles, Echoes of Eternity is not just a memoir but a demonstration of the power of grace, redemption, and the call to a higher spiritual truth.

This book invites readers on a reflective pilgrimage, encouraging them to seek their own spiritual awakening, while offering insight into the universal search for Almighty God across cultural and religious boundaries. Written with the hope of inspiring others to experience the same divine transformation, it is a powerful account of faith in the midst of life's trials.

2. Witnessing to Tribals: Efficacy of COUNT in Indian Missions

Witnessing to Tribals: Efficacy of COUNT in Indian Missions" is a scholarly examination of mission work among tribal communities in India, focusing on the role and effectiveness of a specific strategy or organization known as Christian Outreach Uplifting New Tribes - COUNT. This book delves into the challenges and successes of missionary efforts in reaching out to tribal groups, offering insights into both theoretical and practical aspects of this work. The book emphasizes the importance of strategic frameworks in mission work, particularly in complex and diverse settings like India. It explores the balance between structured methodologies and flexible, context-sensitive approaches.

Dr. Potana offers insightful advice to mission strategists, practitioners, and researchers who want to maximize the effect of their work by conscientizing, incarnationalizing, and teaching pedagogy within a structured framework.

3. Tribals in India: An Anthropo-Missiological Perspective

This book teaches you about the Socio-Political, Economic, and Religious context of the Tribals of South Asia, especially Africa and India. This study investigates the various aspects that influence how tribes in Africa and South Asia are depicted. Dr. Potana unveils tribal Identity, worldviews, Social life, Education, Religion, Culture, Economy, Sickness, Health, and Healing. Christian missionary organizations have a track record of transforming cultures across various nations and continents. Their selfless, transforming mission work in Africa and Asia led to the Socio-Economic liberty of indigenous tribes that come from many backgrounds and cultures. This book plays an important role because it equips mission workers to be relevant and contextual, which is necessary for them to be effective among Tribes in any given country.

4. Old Testament Themes

The book "Old Testament Themes" takes readers on an engrossing journey through the everlasting lessons, copious symbolism, and profound theological concepts found in the Bible. The authors explore the core themes of the books of the Old Testament while also revealing eternal truths about religion, morality, and the human condition. In each chapter of the book, significant theological concepts such as the Suffering Servant, the Lament Psalms, the Theodicy of God, the Transcendence and Immanence of God, and the Justice of God are thoroughly discussed, illustrating their relevance in both historical and contemporary contexts.

This book seeks to enhance the reader's comprehension of these hallowed texts by providing perceptive analysis and captivating exegesis. It also encourages contemplation of the ways in which these themes are relevant in the modern world. This book serves as an invaluable resource that highlights the richness and diversity of Biblical thought, fostering a greater connection to the spiritual heritage that has shaped countless lives across generations, whether for scholars, students, or anyone seeking a greater appreciation of the Old Testament.

5. New Testament Themes

"New Testament Themes" offers a deep and accessible exploration of key theological concepts and practical wisdom found within the New Testament. Each chapter examines significant themes, providing rich historical context, theological insights, and contemporary applications. With a focus on scholarly accuracy and readability, this book invites readers to engage thoughtfully with the enduring truths of the sacred text.

Topics covered include Paul's missionary strategies and their relevance today, the portrayal of Christ in Philippians, and an analysis of the doctrine of election as presented in Romans and Ephesians. It also explores the apocalyptic symbolism in Revelation and the theme of faithfulness in persecution from the

Epistles of Peter, offering valuable insights for readers seeking to apply these teachings in modern contexts.

6. **Theological Themes Volume-1**

This book teaches you about the attributes of God and how to live a life that reflects God's will. Therefore, if you're looking for well-written theological literature, this book fits into your cart because its authors are contemporary missionaries from various backgrounds and cultures who took their subjects seriously and offered theological ideas in a way that was more applicable to real-world situations.

In order to provide the reader with solid evangelical theology, a number of intricate theological themes are interwoven, including The Nature of God, The Communicable Attributes of God, Biblical Inspiration, The Doctrine of Angels, The Doctrine of Trinity, The Doctrine of Salvation, and The Work of the Holy Spirit in a Believer's Life. This book is a component of a brand-new series that captures the changing face of evangelical Christianity. The contributing writers are academicians with a focus on subjects relevant to Evangelical students.

7. Missiological Themes: An Asian Perspective on Christian Mission and Praxis Volume-2

Dr. Potana's book, "Missiological Themes," is quite relevant and necessary. According to David J. Bosch's research, there have been significant paradigm shifts in the theology of Christian missions throughout the church's history. Nevertheless, their cumulative impact could have been better than the 21st century's. A dramatic rethinking of mission has been prompted by various understandings of truth, biblical authority, the nature of non-Christian religions, the role of the local church, the place of social justice, spiritual dynamics, the growth of the majority world church, and many other issues.

As the church entered the third millennium, biblical clarity and global understanding of its purpose grew more and more crucial. The style of writing and treatment of the subject matter of this book will captivate the readers. An astounding amount of highly connected scholarly literature supports and illustrates the subject matter. Dr. Potana has read and studied a large amount of important literature on Missiology.

The concept and structure of the book are both intelligent and engaging. The author's rigorous academic background, combined with his extensive practical missionary field experience, has resulted in a biblically sound and well-balanced literary work on missiology that can enlighten readers and mission practitioners.

8. Missiological Themes: An Asian Perspective on Christian Mission and Praxis, Volume-1

Martin Kahler is steadfast in his claim that 'Mission is the Mother of All Theologies.' Theology cannot exist without missiological studies, even though all theological disciplines profess to include it as a subject. This is the area where a lot of theological colleges fail to thrive—when mission studies are not given the weight they deserve. The lack of emphasis placed on "mission studies" in many theological colleges hinders their prospects of success. The academic theological community marginalizes mission studies, and students of Missiology generally are despised. Throughout history, "Mission Praxis" has been the driving force behind the development of theology. Without 'mission praxis, theology cannot exist, and this has been the case since the first century. There is a serious shortage of scholarly research, literature, and resources for students of 'mission studies' in Asian contexts.

My purpose in writing this book is an attempt to provide comprehensive material related to 'Missiological Themes' in the Asian context. This can be a great resource for students of Missiology who need help getting academic literature on various Missiological Themes.

9. Campus Ministry: A Contextualized Approach

Dr. Venkat Potana's study findings are discussed in this book, making it a helpful tool for sharing the gospel in a multi-faith environment. His extensive research has given the reader enough knowledge to successfully proclaim the Gospel and educate them on the reality of campus ministry.

<u>What Others Say About the Book</u>

"This study reflects Potana's wide experience, insights, and passion for students' ministry. Although academically oriented, it provides significant insights for effective student ministry, especially among the upper castes, Hindus, and Muslims. With a strong combination of academic as well as practical research,

Potana provides a wealth of information with regard to how to do effective student ministry in India. I have known him for a number of years, both as my student and teaching assistant, and I have observed his deep commitment to the cause of mission and evangelism in India. I heartily welcome this book and commend it to all who have a passion to reach the student population in a multi-faith context."

Dr. Atul Y. Aghamkar

Professors of Missiology, SAIACS, Bangalore

Currently, Senior Mission Scholar in Residence at

OMSC

New Haven, CT, USA

"Dr. Venkat Potana's book <u>Campus Ministry: A Contextualize Approach</u> is perhaps a very key book in recreating the passion of witnessing the Gospel to Students with sensitivity with their religious backgrounds in mind. The book is well-researched, and scholarly with historical background of witnessing to students. Dr. Potana not only analyses the ministry of UESI but covers many areas of witnessing, such as the methodologies and contextualization to be relevant to different individuals to whom the Gospel is being communicated. Dr. Venkat is well versed in the actual practices of witnessing as much as the theories. Over the years, I have watched and dialogued with the earnest and enthusiastic Dr. Potana during his research. I have seen many of his approaches in witnessing, especially with relevant contextual approaches in sharing the Gospel, even when he was been the research college doing his PhD. Knowing his heart, approaches and passion makes the book beyond just theories of sharing the Gospel and discipling people. This book is going to be a manual for many who passionately follow the Lord Jesus Christ and share the Gospel with South Asian individuals and communities with relevance and sensitivity. There are many principles to be followed and applied for those who are from other parts of the world. I heartily endorse and recommend this book for light and scholarly reading to be applied on various occasions in witnessing and teaching."

Dr. K. Rajendran,

Associate Director, [Strategic thinking/leadership Development / Global Roundtables],

World Evangelical Alliance Mission Commission. Bangalore, India.

10. Christian Missions Historiography

In *Christian Missions Historiography: An Indian Perspective*, Dr. Venkat Potana offers a fresh and critical reevaluation of how the history of Christian missions has been recorded. This work challenges the dominant Western-centric narrative and presents a balanced perspective, enriching our understanding of Christian historiography through an Indian lens. It delves into how cultural, religious, and political contexts have shaped historical writing over centuries, urging readers to consider the objectivity and methodologies behind historical research.

Ideal for historians, theologians, seminary students, and scholars, this book provides valuable insights into the evaluation of primary and secondary sources. Beyond its focus on Christian missions, it raises larger questions about the influence of context on historiography, making it a must-read for anyone interested in how history is written and interpreted. *Christian Missions Historiography* will encourage readers to think critically about the narratives they encounter and the perspectives that shape them.

11. Shadows Of The Street: India's Street Children

This book delves into the lives of street children, exploring their complex realities through a missiological and literary lens. It engages readers with both compassion and intellectual depth, offering fresh insights into global street child ministries. The work draws from a blend of firsthand experiences, research, and the poignant use of stories, making it accessible to scholars, ministry leaders, and anyone interested in social justice. Each page unravels narratives of resilience, illustrating the vital role of faith-based missions and literature in addressing the plight of street children.

The book stands out by examining street children not just as statistics but as individuals with stories that intersect with faith, culture, and society. Through carefully crafted chapters, the author examines missiological strategies and highlights how literature has portrayed street children over the years. It bridges academic rigor with heartfelt storytelling, encouraging readers to reflect on the power of compassion, community outreach, and advocacy for the marginalized.

If you're interested in learning about effective ways to engage with vulnerable youth, or you are looking for a resource that blends academic inquiry with practical ministry advice, Shadows is a compelling choice. Its insightful approach to missiology and children's literature offers practical tools for those involved in missions, outreach, and community service. This book will deepen your understanding of how street children can be empowered through faith-based initiatives, and inspire you to take action.

12. Indigenous Missions in India

This book is meant to be a squeaky wheel to bring up the issue of Indigenous Missions in India. It also reflects the Author's wide experience, insights, and passion for the Mission of God. This factual and figurative presentation is going to be a manual for all those who passionately follow the teachings of Lord Jesus Christ meaningfully to the South Asian individuals and communities with relevance and sensitivity so that they could undergo a spiritual rebirth and pave their way towards revealing the Divine.

This is one of the outstanding books to understand the indigenous missions in India. This book is well-designed and balances the combined structure of theory and field research. While reading this book, you will find recommendations that can help to set a new direction for undertaking better ways of the liberation of the oppressed in twenty-first-century India. Your dimension of understanding of the mission will be enhanced, and you will get a new perspective. Dr. Potana is an academic research scholar who has done much research at the grassroots level and he has also shown missionary burden for the people. He has applied this methodology in reaching out to them.